BEYOND DREAMING

A Guide to Astral Projection

Gene Hart

Awakening Consciousness & Journeying Into Multidimensional Realities That Exist Beyond The Dream State

ISBN: 9798713213923

This book is dedicated to every person who bravely follows their heart into the mysteries of reality, and to my dear friend Vicente, who opened my eyes to the power of sacrifice for others, and to my wife, Innes, who showed me how to speak to my truth.

As light illuminates the dark, may your awareness expand brightly to make the unknown, known.

CONTENTS

Disclaimer

In this book, I have compiled tips and advice which attempt to shine light on various frequently asked questions I've received from hundreds of people; it seeks to address common struggles shared by many. Please keep in mind that these are my personal suggestions, drawn from conclusions I've made from my own experience; they may not apply to everyone.

The goal here is not to convince anyone that the phenomena of OBEs are real, nor are they to challenge anyone's beliefs. The multidimensional universe is simply a reality of nature which we can all experience directly, regardless of belief. This book aims to share my findings with those interested and to help them experience it themselves.

I don't promise that the information here will guarantee to fix anything you're currently struggling with or that it will suddenly give you out-of-body experiences; while that's certainly possible, it's ultimately up to you. At best, I'm inviting you to read my perspectives and contemplate them with your own intuition; as a result, this should complement and inspire your own practice.

At the end of the book, I have provided my email address where you can contact me if you have any questions. I welcome both sceptics and believers with open arms.

Good luck on your journey!

INTRODUCTION

The primary purpose of this book is for others to learn how to awaken consciousness, on top of this, to also direct this awakening towards the realities of lucid dreaming and out of body experiences, comprehending them in a direct and tangible way, as opposed to intellectual speculation or belief.

For anyone picking up this book entirely new to these topics, lucid dreaming is the experience of being in a dream and, at the same time, being aware of being in the dream.

Try this little exercise; remember any dream that you had at any point in your life, replay the dream in your memory, but this time, imagine you suddenly become aware that you are in the dream. Look around in wonder at the power of your subconscious mind to create such a convincing environment and narrative for you to just moments ago be fooled by. This is the magnificent and insightful power of lucid dreaming; to be able to study your own inner subconscious workings, submerged in a direct, eye-opening and introspective experience. In such an experience, you can control, manipulate and create whatever you like; your imagination is your only limit. You can explore what your mind is creating and even ask it and the dream characters around you why they are doing what they are doing and what they represent. It is a profoundly personal and influential way to know oneself. In this sense, dreams are a significant part of our own spiritual growth. Consequently, lucid dreaming is a natural and essential part of the path towards realising out of body experiences (OBEs).

On the other hand, an out of body experience is an experience where you perceive and feel yourself separate and detach from your physical body, entering into an objective non-physical dimension. This dimension can often be parallel to your physical location. This notoriously happens when your physical body is sleeping peacefully in bed.

One way to get an idea of how an OBE may feel is by looking around your surroundings where you are right now. Try to imagine for a moment that where you are right now, physically reading this book, is actually in another dimension and that your physical body is fast asleep somewhere else - really look around and consider how 'real' your seemingly physical environment feels; now try to amplify this feeling of 'realness' by one hundred times. This is a glimpse of what astral projection feels like; it feels just like being in physical waking life, and it can often feel more real and closer to reality than the physical dimension. In fact, it is commonly known amongst experienced practitioners that it can feel so blisteringly tangible that when you wake up, it can give the sensation that physical life is actually more like a dream in comparison. That is how influential OBEs can be on our sense of perception.

OBEs takes place not in a dream of your own creation but in an actual location within a non-physical dimension, it is not affected by your subconscious mind like a dream, and you can't control the environment in the same way. It is an actual place where you can explore any part of Earth or the cosmos with your own direct senses. You can have conversations with other people, and you can even travel into the past or future. OBEs happen in the astral plane, which is beyond time and space. This book will explore some of these sub-topics and look deeper into the difference between lucid dreams and OBEs (astral projection). Understanding the difference is a fundamental part of appreciating and understanding these non-physical experiences.

Astral projection implies an awakening to new states of consciousness. It has far-reaching long-term consequences, such as a much deeper understanding of reality, a more objective perception in daily life, and a new sense of existence itself, which has also famously led many to transcend their fear of death.

The term 'astral projection' is simply another way to describe an out of body experience. The main difference is that the term 'out of body experience' is more commonly used amongst conventional discussions, including being recognised within medical communities, especially when relating it to near-death experiences. The term 'astral projection' is more widely used within spiritual communities to describe the spiritual practice of consciously and intentionally coming out of the body. In this book, we are essentially studying how to have conscious out of body experiences; so, the two terms are the same thing.

Astral projection also has the word 'Astral' in it, which denotes what has been spiritually recognised for centuries as the plane that exists parallel, or beyond, the physical plane. These planes are non-physical, complex and multidimensional in nature, just as consciousness is. There are some encouraging scientific breakthroughs, especially amongst quantum physics, which seem to be on the verge of discovering these planes or dimensions of reality, which have also been recognised for centuries by several spiritual communities and 'enlightened masters' in different cultures and time periods. For example, modern quantum physicists have suggested that there exists eleven dimensions. Similarly, in esoteric teachings, which explore the ‘Kabbalah’, you will find eleven dimensions of nature. However, we won't be exploring the countless connections between modern scientific breakthroughs of the non-physical and esoteric teachings; there is much information on that already; you will find it if you wish to seek it. If you have picked up this book, then I assume you already understand some of this, and that you've somewhat moved past the level of speculation and 'connecting the dots' and that you now want to experience the reality of this for yourself directly. If not, don't worry; if you sincerely want to experience OBEs for yourself, then it will all make sense with time, practice and experience.

Alas, I am no master, and I'm not looking for followers. When I say that I'm teaching 'awakening', it does not imply that people can be only either 'awakened' or 'not awakened', that would be reflective of conventional two-dimensional thinking. The process of awakening is multidimensional and has thousands of layers of degrees to it. We are all more or less awakened to a certain degree, some more than others. The main problem is that on a scale compared to the infinite potential of awakening, most people are a long way from a significant amount of awakening where it can positively affect their material and spiritual lives, especially when it comes to having conscious out of body experiences.

I have been experiencing OBE phenomena for over ten years, and only up until recently, amidst the COVID-19 pandemic, did I begin to share my experiences and knowledge publicly. I know that speaking of such topics often ends in ridicule, yet I have written this book in an act of humility and service to others; I'm simply reporting my findings in the hope that others, who are interested, can benefit from it. I'm selling this book not for profit but at an affordable price so that anyone with a few pennies can buy it. I personally do not advocate for extortionate prices and profiting off something that should be taught free in schools. The knowledge of astral projection is a natural birthright for every human being. I only have one sincere wish; for you to have the authentic experience of coming out of your body with all your senses and full waking awareness intact, just as you are right now reading this book. Astral projection is not frightening or complicated but a natural, liberating, and sublime experience that leaves your soul only longing for more - and ultimately changes your view on death and the afterlife in deeply impactful ways that you never previously considered possible.

There are many studies on the phenomena of OBEs already. If you are interested in such things, I recommend the book, 'Leaving the Body' by Scott Rogo. Also, look into Graham Nicholls, who has had thousands of experiences, verified them with witnesses in scientific settings and is also being actively tested on; he is one-hundred percent scientific in his approach.

Nevertheless, what one may realise is, and what my personal advice is, is that even though modern science is accelerating at a relatively fast pace in new technology and discoveries, it is still somewhat in a stone age era compared to what there is yet to be discovered. Instead of relying on these groups of people for answers, what we can do as an alternative is become courageous and self-willed enough to become our own pioneers and delve into the anatomy of consciousness and reality for ourselves, through direct experience, and report back our findings to those who are open to it; just as I am doing with you.

For some people, astral projection will be just to experience the novel of it. My perspective on this is that although yes, it is a 'cool' and an exciting experience, the novel and experience of astral projection doesn't always benefit us spiritually. Waking physical experience and meditation can actually help our progress more than astral projection at times. So, my point is, I firmly believe astral projection should be integrated as part of our individual spiritual growth and awakening. When we approach it in this way, we have much more insightful and profound experiences, helping us grow as souls and eventually helping others in the process too. If you are currently only having short and blurry experiences, don't worry; every experience is useful practice. Try to find or learn the meaning from all of your experiences.

THE BACKGROUND OF LIFE

As a child, I was not often concerned with what school teachers had to say. Instead, I'd be more fascinated with an insect walking across my table or what the other children were doing or thinking. I often had my eyes gazing out the window, letting my mind run wild with the infinite possibilities of what could happen at any given moment. Perhaps an asteroid could hit the Earth, or what if everyone suddenly developed superpowers, or I'd consider what it would be like flying amongst a flock of birds I saw. I grew up with adults telling me that I wasn't 'academic', but the truth is, I wasn't interested in surface-level conversations that had no meaning to what was happening around me in the present moment; I was more concerned with the background of life rather than the foreground. For example, I'd keenly notice the shapes of clouds or count how many trees were in a field, or more notably, I'd notice the impression a person gave me long before seeing what they were doing or what they were saying.

When I did pay 'proper' academic attention, it would be in subjects such as science or art; science which promised some explanation to the mysteries of life, and art which let me undertake activities without another odd intellectual lesson to regurgitate. Alas, this is the purity of a child's mind. Now here we are, older, buying books and guides trying to figure out something so natural and straightforward; how to separate consciousness from the body.

Yet, many of us cannot grasp this innate capacity for non-physical exploration, which is all but second nature to liberated awareness. This is simply the practice; to liberate awareness from the self-limiting beliefs and perceptions we impose on it. We have to learn how we learned about how we perceive the world and then carefully proceed to unlearn that which no longer serves a purpose for our personal freedom.

One of the main reasons we struggle with astral projection is that we have become so used to intellectually scrutinising everything we learn. In typical modern society, we tend to study every topic's foreground, asking every question that appears on the mind's surface-level relating it to everything we already proudly understand about physical existence; we are rarely concerned about the background - understanding things critically and fundamentally. For some people, they do this to a terrifying extent. For example, if you ask them, "What is the Sun?" they will answer with frightening confidence something like, "The Sun is a star which is made up of hot plasma caused by nuclear fusion reactions." On a superficial scientific layer, this is true, yet it is far from a description that would best suit the Sun's infinitely far more profound reality. Sadly, for this type of individual, all they see when they look up at the Sun is a description in their mind, never stopping for one moment to gaze at its beauty which sings more words than any scientific description could offer. I am not saying such definitions or beliefs are bad or wrong to hold; I'm saying that if you don't understand that it's not reflective of the actual essence of the Sun, for example, then you have not realised a deeper dimension of life that goes transcendentally beyond any sort of shabby description.

There are so many different examples of this type of defective way of perceiving the world. I commonly see it when people become interested in out of body travel. For instance, when someone discovers the concept of astral projection, they usually ask questions such as, "When out of body, how do I travel to another country if I don't know the way? Do I need a map?", "How do I pass through physical objects?" or "Isn't it all just a figment of my imagination?" and the best one; "Isn't astral projection just lucid dreaming?" I say the best one because we have so many assumptions, connotations, and preconceptions about 'dreaming' in conventional modern knowledge. It may not seem like there's anything wrong with these questions at first glance; however, they are filled with deep-rooted assumptions embedded in our perception of how we think the world works on the surface layer of reality.

When trying to have out of body experiences, people often overthink the process in the same ways we conventionally think of learning new things. They do this by dissecting every step and asking questions such as, "When I get to such-and-such a stage, how do I proceed to the next stage?" or "Do I need to have my chakras activated before astral projecting?". In this book, I hope to explain to you a state of being where you can rely not on complicated theories and speculations, but instead on your own inner guidance and intuition, which favours your ability to trust the flow of your own natural processes rather than your apprehensions. One can study the piano for many years, but it takes feeling the keys and the beat of the music to play it. Learning astral projection, which barely relies on thought, is understood not through theory but through experience and practice. There will be a series of exercises provided throughout the book which you can use. The rest of the book should act to complement your contemplation and understanding.

Accordingly, astral projection is the only subject I've felt is discernible enough for me to write a book on. Just as I've felt since I was a child, I've found little personal purpose in pursuing subjects that don't have practical application in my personal life. Some may notice I put little stress on backing up my claims or accounts of my own out of body experiences. The purpose of this book is not to convince you that out of body experiences are real but to guide those who are ready and open to the possibility of the experience. With that said, I do my best to point you to the truth of what I'm conveying, not based on scientific data or fanciful ancient texts but through logical reasoning based on my own direct experience since I was eighteen years old, which is when I started this path and began having these experiences. I am not one of those much heard about astral projectors who started doing it naturally since they were children; in fact, when I started out, I was far from living a spiritual life, depressed and did not know about anything spiritual. It was only amidst a 'lost' stage of my life that I started to seek the spiritual dimension. One thing led to another, and I began to diligently approach and investigate astral projection and learned how to do it gradually, just as anyone can do.

Ultimately, I or anyone else cannot convince you of this incredible ability to journey into other dimensions, and only you can open that door within yourself. This book is mainly for those seeking the authentic experience of coming out of body, also known as astral projection, which is also essentially the same experience as near-death experiences. At the same time, this book will still be helpful for experienced practitioners; as any well-versed practitioner knows, it is always beneficial to maintain your interest and inspiration in this topic. Every author often has their own distinctive kind of eloquence and insight into these matters, for we are all immeasurably unique sparks of essence deriving from the same source, benefitting each other in different ways.

When one begins to awaken their consciousness, their light shines a hundred times more than it had before, like a flower blooming for others to marvel at its artistry. For every true spiritual master who has lived on this planet, you will find boundless wisdom, all as unique and insightful as the other, but in their core, their essence, you can always sense that one same source from which they all speak from. This source is already in your life, it is what gives you the drive to chase your desires, to get up and work every day, to marry the one you love, but this boundless energy we receive we often have little control over, and unconsciousness can enter our lives, often leading to decisions we don't necessarily want to make; including in our dreams at night. Consequently, the average person does not remember their dreams, because they are not making the decisions, the subconscious, or unconscious, is. This source, this deeper core of ourselves, is what we need to illuminate so that we can understand it more profoundly. In this way, we help ourselves realise the barriers that stand in our way of living consciously; in our waking lives, *and* in our sleeping lives.

Some readers will desire no hint of backing up any of the claims I make in this book, for they have already glimpsed the palpability and immensity of other dimensions themselves. Others may have a more challenging time understanding. To those I say, if you have the desire to stick with it, from some unknown urge within you, then I encourage you to be patient and let the ideas and feelings flow through you and follow them naturally; there is no need to overthink any of the topics explored in this book or to take them too seriously, nor to think fearfully about them either. If you have picked up this book, then it's likely that a shift has already begun within you, and on an intellectual level, you may have no idea what is going on - this is fine; you'll eventually begin to be comfortable with 'not knowing', and only then will the answers and experiences begin to flow. The realisation of one's own ignorance is the beginning of authentic self-knowledge.

"I am the wisest man alive, for I know one thing, and that is that I know nothing."

- *Socrates*

Additionally, you will find some beneficial practices throughout this book that will help you align more clearly to your inner awakening and get better direct knowledge of yourself and what is happening. As you read the book, you may experience more vivid dreams, come to more profound realisations in your waking life, and perhaps make spontaneous decisions you wish you always had or thought you never would. Whatever happens, trust the process; this is the grace of living in a harmonious relationship with your inner and outer experience and in a higher level of consciousness.

Suppose you're experiencing changes occurring which you never made any plans on doing on an egoic level. In that case, you can be fairly confident that they are most likely happening for good reason and as part of your spiritual growth. Those reasons can only be discovered and understood when we make the effort of looking within. Decisions and intent made by the egoic parts of ourselves can often be unsure, fickle and uninformed, leading to undesirable situations and a blurrier way of life. Whereas intentions made by a deeper part of us, our consciousness, our *Being*, is usually aligned with our best interest, leading to happiness and clarity. The same goes for astral projection; we need to follow our gut and heart instead of our head. Even scientific studies have proven that there are central neurons in the heart and gut; the heart actually sends more signals to the brain than the brain sends in return. Thus, spiritual knowledge is held in our cells and DNA, not in some imagined idealistic worldviews.

It is also important to point out that there is no need to over-scrutinise anything in his book to the point where it makes you suffer or doubt life even more. Astral projection is nothing short of life-affirming, especially in comparison to purely materialistic perspectives. Astral projection is about going beyond all perspectives to find a closer version of the ultimate truth to reality. Naturally, through experiencing it, one's perspectives will start to lean towards less materialistic values.

When seemingly realising certain truths, I've known some people who have become depressed, including myself in my early days on this path, such as the thought that your entire life is all but a dream, or perhaps in some out of body experience, you discover some reality about your ego that you don't like. The truth is rarely what we think it will be, but what is the better way to live? To carry on living in delusion or to be honest and recognise the truth when we discover it? Let me please firmly state that this book's primary purpose is for the awakening of consciousness; that is to say, for you to wake up and realise the many truths of reality within every moment of your life and to understand every aspect of your existence, in your waking life as well as when you're asleep. Let me stress that the expansion of higher consciousness is a sublime and transcendental experience that emanates from the core of reality and the core of our *Being*. It is enlightening, awe-inspiring, and changes how you perceive and experience life - the way we always should; full and overflowing with joy, wisdom, and unconditional love for all that is.

Specific subjects in this book will be more challenging for me to back up rationally. If you have a strong disposition against the reality of other dimensions existing beyond the physical plane, then perhaps this guide on how to experience them directly is not for you. However, be mindful that I welcome believers and sceptics alike to try what I know is natural for every living being. I sincerely hope that out of body travel will be taught and practised in schools one day, or at least on how to access and explore similar states of consciousness.

So, keep an open mind; ultimately, the universe is essentially a pure mystery, this mystery wherein lies the heart of its intelligence. How infinitely intelligent must the universe be to create the human mind with its vastness and power, which has a hold of our collective and individual lives so intensely?

"The most beautiful thing we can experience is the mysterious. It is the source of all true art and science. He to whom the emotion is a stranger, who can no longer pause to wonder and stand wrapped in awe, is as good as dead; his eyes are closed."

- *Albert Einstein*

Throughout the book, my use of quotes isn't to convince you of certain aspects through the credibility of notable people of the past but to elaborate on what I'm endeavouring to transmit. It has always been a great challenge for any author to accurately describe spiritual dimensions that exist beyond time, space and conventional wisdom; spoken human language is all but a vain attempt to describe the indescribable. The mind is continuously labelling and assuming every process, but OBEs have little to do with the intellect. In reality, it is as easy as walking, breathing or learning to ride a bike. When learning to ride a bike, should the child keep asking their parents endless questions, or should they just get up and keep trying? The more questions the child asks, the more confused and overcomplicated they may make the process; this is the state of mind of many today trying to learn the fine art of meditation and separating consciousness from the body.

We cannot treat astral travel in the same way as treating it like a university degree, assigning every process with complicated concepts to dissect cerebrally; it *has* to be felt and *experienced* by your *Being*. By *Being,* I mean the feeling of being present, in your core, as opposed to *thinking*; 'thinking' being phenomena that occurs separately to *Being*. 'Being' is the silent awareness that is essentially *you*, it does nothing, yet it is everything. It is the silent observer that always been in your life.

Astral travel is a level of consciousness that is beyond logical reasoning, at least for now. I do believe scientific organisations will one day be able to study it with more accuracy, but in the meantime, modern science is far from such a feat.

If I were to teach a class of children and a class of adults about how to come out of body, the children would most likely have double the adults' success rate. Children are far less likely to be cut off from their *Being* due to excessive thinking that adults usually adopt as we grow in modern society. One crucial factor that you will see me emphasise regularly is that conscious out of body experiences do not require thought; it is a way of *Being*, a level of consciousness free from attachment to physical-sensory-experience. Out of body experiences are as natural as learning how to breathe; it is instinctual, primal and intrinsic to the very core of every person.

AWAKENING

Naturally, the curious child I once was finally grew older, and I left school with average grades. However, I became one of the most successful amongst people I knew, opening many businesses and gaining a lot of work experience. Although I had little interest in school, I had always been practical and have always kept busy, putting in over 70 hours a week into businesses. This practicality in my nature clearly came as an advantage when it came to approaching meditation and astral projection.

I was also accepted into one of the most prestigious universities in the UK to study Computer Science. Proud of my achievement, I attended the course, ravishing in the accomplishment that the world had told me was so important. Nevertheless, one month into university lectures, the looming tendency to not pay attention to the excessive and meaningless academia which had engrossed me so profoundly as a child was still there as an adult, and with great dissatisfaction, I quit the course.

With material purpose dissolving in my life, I found a deep interest in lucid dreaming, and I spent the next year engrossed in it. With the distraction of academic information out of the way, I found I had far more energy to focus on personal endeavours. This was when I began my personal path of discovery; the first topic that I developed a genuine interest in was lucid dreaming.

When I studied and practised it, I found myself naturally having hundreds of lucid dreams. This sense of being awake within my subconscious mind was fascinating, and I had never been more passionate than in any other subject than this. It wasn't just something I could intellectually hypothesise about but something I could experience, feel and touch.

Lucid dreaming captivated me, a possibility to escape this mundane world and do what I want in a world of my own with infinite possibilities, and that's just what I did; I went on to have hundreds of enjoyable and entertaining lucid dreams. I flew through worlds of my own imagination, and I spoke with my subconscious to better understand myself and my fears. I even practised the guitar while I was asleep.

Nonetheless, I mistakingly treated lucid dreaming as a form of escapism, which was ultimately unsatisfying. As usual, I was still asking what the purpose behind all of this was.

I enjoyed it for some time and learned many things about myself, but back then, I was still somewhat depressed and unsatisfied about the world and life's meaning in general. Eventually, I became bored with lucid dreaming. I asked myself, "What was the point in experiencing life if all that I ever experience is in my mind?", this question didn't just address my dreams, but also my waking life because, through lucid dreaming, I came to the realisation that everything we see, even when awake, is only a reflection of our mind. When we see cars, trees and other people, etc., we usually see the labels and ideas in our mind that we attach to them. With this somewhat grim realisation of the 'virtualness' of life, I gained an interest in meditation as a way to find some hope and meaning behind it all.

Later in life, I eventually graduated with a Philosophy degree. However, I was still mostly dissatisfied with what I had experienced academically. Western philosophy topics were interesting, but they were mainly explored with open-ended questions, deriving from unenlightened western philosophers, who, like me, questioned reality yet never seemed to find any answers. Dissatisfied and disenchanted by philosophy, religion, and disgruntled by science, I still felt somewhat hollow. I knew so much about the surface layer of perception and reality, but if I was honest, I still lacked some sort of fulfilling substance. I could develop attractive philosophical thoughts about the world. However, deep down, I still knew something was missing. What was the point in continuing to live if I could not find the meaning behind the mundaneness of life that I had felt so strongly as a child? I reclused myself into depression throughout this stage of life.

I continued to persevere with meditation, and I eventually came to the realisation that I lived within the self-created illusion of my own mind. Through this realisation, I came to understand that I was missing one essential ingredient: actively expanding consciousness, which has the ability to help us let go and free ourselves of perceptions that no longer serve us. Consciousness is the intelligent awareness that observes our thoughts, which is beyond all the ideas and labels of ourselves and the world. Thus, since it is greater than all that, it provides a space to transcend them.

Once one's awareness is submerged within consciousness rather than the labyrinth of the mind, one begins to have liberating and enlightening shifts in awareness. That's when I conveniently found out about astral projection. I got my first book on the matter, 'The Art & Practice of Astral Projection by Ophiel'. I practised what the book told me to religiously with nothing better to do in my empty life. I put all of my depression to one side and gave my all into giving life the benefit of the doubt that there was more to it than what speculating philosophers and unenlightened sciences imply so often.

Through diligent practice, I found the instinctual '*way of Being*' needed for astral projection. That is, to gain control over my mind through peaceful silence and stop dreaming, in other words, to stop constantly projecting my own illusions of the world into my awareness.

One night while lying in bed, I was in for a shocking surprise; I had my first out of body experience. For the first time in my life, I had indeed found something which did not disappoint or leave me with a sense of dissatisfaction or more looming questions. I had peeked through the veil of physical illusion and perception, which usually grips our consciousness to the material world so firmly. It was pure joy, and I was in a glow of awe for many days.

Lucid dreaming, meditation, and astral projection all have distinctive layers of awakening and profundities, both while having out of body experiences and also after waking up. After coming out of my body for the first time, I had spontaneous and powerful occasions where I would be weeping in waking life from existential realisations of joy and enlightenment. My depression was being healed.

My First Out-of-Body Experience

25th July 2011

One night, I found myself waking up in the middle of my sleep. However, instead of waking up regularly, I stayed still and immediately began spontaneously feeling trembling vibrations all over my body, like an earthquake; I started to see colours swirling in my vision through my closed eyelids. I heard noises, like a mix of a hurricane and white noise. All of these extrasensory phenomena became so intense that I eventually began to have the feeling that I could 'lean into them' and separate from my physical body, and thus I floated upwards. It was a slow and intense separation. As I gradually detached, I saw my physical body fast asleep beneath me. This new type of ghost-like body, which I had never experienced before, felt acutely energetic; as if I was on the constant descent of a rollercoaster whilst having continual electrical goosebumps. I felt blisteringly alive, but at the same time, heavy and more real than anything I had ever experienced before in my waking life, and definitely more palpable and 'physical' than any of the hundreds of lucid dreams I had beforehand. I felt the weight of my energetic body lower to my bedroom floor, and I felt the tactual sensation of the carpet under my feet. I looked around my dark lit room, which felt more natural and vivid than I'd ever seen before; it had a luminous and magical quality to it. I was awestruck, especially because this was nothing like the countless lucid dreams I had before this. I was indeed separate from my physical body and brain as I observed it sleeping in my bed; there was truly no doubt of this.

My environment clearly had an independent existence of its own; I barely felt the possibility of manipulating the environment, which is so easy and natural in lucid dreams. I examined my room; the moonlight through the window cast shadows on the floor and wall. I moved my hands slowly in and out of the moonlight and touched my bedroom wall. I saw it in blisteringly shocking detail. I had never seen my wall and hands in such a fresh and realistic way before. It was strange to think that all of this felt highly physical, yet I knew it was in the non-physical.

When we successfully astral project, it's like we have a stronger cushion protecting us from thoughts entering and ruining the experience with its labels, and we are left with only pure uninterrupted experience; with a vividness alike to taking a psychedelic drug without actually consuming one, and without any of the 'brain-fog' or 'drunkness' that such substances induce; it is an entirely sober experience with your usual day-to-day awareness in-tact. Consequently, you are left with a hyper-aware state of perception with a foundation in a familiar and calm sense of yourself. Yet, you are 'out of my mind', and 'out of body' - you are consciousness.

The authenticity of the experience was so overwhelming

and convincing that I amusingly had the instinctual habit of being careful not to wake up anyone in the house while I walked around, if that was even possible. I felt so normal and my usual self that I considered whether I would die or how I would get back inside my body. Usually, these types of thoughts cut the experience short for most people, but through meditation, I had adequate control over not letting such thoughts consume me.

Getting a hold of myself, I intended to go outside. With the knowledge that this dimension was ultimately non-physical, I flew through my bedroom wall and came out hovering on the other side to see a beautiful clear night sky with a full moon shining its light on the lush treetops. I had never seen outside my mundane house with such a spiritual and magical quality before. It was visually stunning, but what's more was the sense of vibrancy, life and emotion that emitted from everything I saw.

I became so overwhelmed with what I was seeing that I woke up. I was in a state of shock and didn't go back to sleep that night. However, I was also overjoyed. I truly felt as though I had found some hidden treasure, stored on the edge of reality, located parallel to the physical dimension. This feeling has never really left me, and this sense of joy I always feel with every OBE, it is hard to not fall in love with such an experience.

I got up, struggling to contain my excitement; I wrote down the experience in my journal, desperately trying to express in words the tangibility of it. As I did, I looked at my room and how it was precisely the same as how I'd just experienced it. I went to my bedroom window to wave my hands through the moonlight and got shivers feeling how different it felt to do this physically; it somehow felt less vibrant. I wanted to be back in that dimension. The physical now felt like more of a dream, and to this day, I have rarely felt any different. However, I have learned that living more present in waking life can give almost the same quality as the astral plane.

Afterwards, I left my bedroom and quietly went outside the door to see just how everything was exactly the same as I had seen, with the clear night sky and full moon shining its light on the treetops.

I failed to sleep after this. I couldn't wait to tell loved ones what I had discovered. I felt born again, and ever since, I have never felt life in the same way. After eighteen years of wondering what was behind this all, I had finally discovered the verge of something which clearly had extraordinary and meaningful potential to investigate. If I was able to access a world that was beyond the physicality of matter, what else could I discover through it?

When I told loved ones, to my disappointment, I could see their uninterest, bewilderment and scepticism. If only I could shake them out of their dream-like state and show them it was real. It took some time for me to realise that telling people who aren't interested has little use. I'm sure this has been the heartfelt struggle of almost every person who has come to the same realisation. Today, I believe awakening happens when people are ready, and even then, it is usually a gradual and gentle process.

The exciting afterglow of this experience faded a little, and I continued my devoted meditation practice in a disciplined and profound way for many weeks. As well as the many OBEs that occurred, I also had multiple experiences in physical waking life where I would feel overflowed with pure conscious awareness. The path of astral projection clearly does not just affect our experience in sleep but also has profound effects on our waking lives.

This direct experience of out of body consciousness can be challenging to understand if you haven't experienced it for yourself. Still, you can get a taste of it through persistent and consistent meditation. It is a feeling of freedom away from the noise of the mind, which derives from an arising of inner peace and practical understanding. One specific experience I had spontaneously happened when I decided to go for a walk one day.

An Overflow of Presence in the Physical

15th August 2011

I walked through lush green paths which were behind my house. As I did often back then, I walked mindfully, and like a Buddhist monk, I did my best to not engage in thoughts or emotions that would distract me from focusing on every single step I took, and also from connecting with the nature around me. I was enjoying my walk; my mind was that of a Zen student, impartial but highly aware, non-labelling but acutely discerning. As I walked down one path, a mother with a baby in her pram was walking in my direction, and as they went past me, I spontaneously seemed to have reached an inner threshold. I was flooded with one of the most sublime feelings I have ever had while in the physical. To my shock, some kind of energy, call it the aura of a mother and her baby, had crescendoed a sort of surrendering of my 'egoic wall of perception', giving way for only the sacred intelligence of my heart and awareness to operate unhindered and untainted. My emotions, which I thought I had under perfect control beforehand, suddenly burst like an erupting geyser. Within seconds I flooded with tears as my whole experience opened up to me as if all the walls of my perception had suddenly collapsed; the reality I was now perceiving was singing a beautiful chorus into all my senses.

Everything I looked at was new, vibrant and full of life. The sounds of birds and everything around me was so pure and innocent, I felt I had been given new ears of super-hearing abilities. I looked around me, raptured in awe as if I had awakened from a dream. I could suddenly see the sun's rays in the air and how its loving luminosity penetrated everything it touched, including how my body absorbed its life-giving essence. The lavish nature around me suddenly became animated with life as I noticed every leaf sway in the wind. If I paid closer attention to a tree or flower, I could have sworn I became aware of its recognition of me. I realised for a moment how strange I must have looked to people, I was on a usually busy path in the middle of the day, but I did not care. Surprisingly though, there was nobody else on the path that day, and I didn't bump into anyone in this entire experience as if the world was saying, 'this is just for you'. I had been seeking some sort of answers to life through my devoted meditation practices for months, and if I were to discover anything, it would be in this indescribable new state of consciousness that had spontaneously risen in me, where the world had seemed to expose its naked soul. This was beyond thought, beyond questioning, the intellectual mind had given up with tempting me for attention, and the logical part of me seemed to have entirely shut down.

I carried on walking, absorbing this newfound state, and eventually found a bench in a small park. I sat and observed the tree leaves moving in the wind and watched all the squirrels and birds around me in nothing short of pure, ecstatic joy. I don't know how long I sat on that park bench, but time did not seem to have an influence in this state. All I know is many hours passed until I got up. My consciousness had moved to a dimension beyond time and space, which only existed in uninterrupted bliss with the clear realisation that the illusion of separateness was just a fallacy in our usual perception. I *felt* rather than *saw* things; and whatever I looked at, I felt an inner knowing that resonated throughout my entire *Being*. In this way, I could appreciate everything from a bird to a tree or even a single blade of grass; complemented with an underlying *knowing* that the consciousness I usually experience is no different from the awareness that is rooted in any other life forms' essence. In ultimate reality, everything is one.

Such is a spontaneous awakening of consciousness that can happen by grace when we make efforts to meditate, and gives us glimpses of 'higher' types of awareness. This type of awakening can spontaneously occur not just in the physical plane but also in the astral plane.

Since this happened, the feeling passed somewhat, but it never entirely disappeared, and it has always been there in the background, or it surfaces again when I'm in meditation or go for long walks in nature. This spontaneous and personal event of awakening has always been a profound frame of reference when I've felt a little imbalanced or needed answers. Our language does not have enough words to describe such an experience; what I felt in those moments was a powerful expansion of love - love being the blissful emotion of the body that naturally arises when the mind surrenders to reality, rather than trying to constantly conjure up its own dream realities instead. When you reach such a state in meditation, you realise that 'love' is your natural state and not something that needs to be 'found'. It is only really 'found' when you let go and allow yourself to stop adding your own narrative to life, to *what is*.

This is why love can come in many forms in life, because different things have the ability to make our minds still enough so that we can perceive closer to that truer reality of 'oneness'; whether it be a loving partner, pets, children, beautiful scenery in nature, a hobby etc. Such things can help us reach that inner tranquillity in life, but it's also important to note that we need not rely on external things or people for such states. We can connect to those states through meditation and our relationship with ourselves.

Through tapping into that source of love within, we unleash a divine source of energy to live by which benefits all living beings, rather than relying on other people for our peace of mind, which ultimately leads to suffering and attachment to physical form. Remember, our goal towards astral projection involves not clinging to physical reality and the objects in it, whether it be material possessions, loved ones or anything else. This is not to say we should remove such things from our life, but it means that those external things have no power to create any more drama or suffering in our lives anymore, because we generate our own source of power from within.

> "When the mind stops searching, when it stops wanting refuge, when it no longer goes in search of security, when it no longer craves more books and information, when it ignores even the memory of desire, only then will Love arrive within."
>
> - *Samael Aun Weor*

As my meditation grew and continued in my life, my out of body experiences started to become more profound as well. This next experience was the first time I realised that people truly did live in the astral plane in the afterlife:

Earth-like Afterlife

2nd July 2012

I woke up in the middle of the night into a state of well-being after a relaxing, meditative evening. Out of habit, I focused on falling back to sleep with full waking awareness. In the depths of my heavy slumber, unusual sounds began to present themselves; loud banging, vibrating and people speaking. My physical eyes opened involuntarily, and the sounds ceased. I relaxed and closed my eyes again, and they returned. If I keenly focused my attention on them, they would disappear, so I let them be. They seemed to develop in intensity until they had consumed my full awareness naturally. In the same way, a convulsion emanating from my stomach started to engulf my body; I began to vibrate intensely while simultaneously having the excruciating sensation of falling or flying.

Hypnagogic colours began to swirl into my vision. They seemed to be struggling to form an image. As I focused, I found myself emerging into a scene. I felt groggy as if I had just woken up. I knew immediately I was somewhere else out of body. I found myself sitting in a meditative lotus position in the middle of a stairway of a large building. My surroundings were grey and dull. Sitting next to me was a man. He felt familiar, and a part of me recognised him as a friend, but not someone I knew in waking life; perhaps he was from a past life, or someone which only a multidimensional part of me knew. We spoke for a while, but I only remember the last part of the conversation.

"We will go up the stairs together," he said.

A woman who I wasn't previously aware was with us stood in front of me and abruptly said, "We would expect you to go higher".

Before having any time to analyse her, two small spheres, which were vertically connected by a 'cord' in-between, appeared above her head. Each sphere displayed an image inside; I focused on the top one, and I began to zoom into it. The scene of this stairway began to fade. I had a moment of apprehension. I did not want to wake up and ruin what I felt was some 'transportation' to another place. For an instant, I held onto the man's arm in an attempt to stay grounded. I soon found myself back in bed. On reflection, I thought that the experience was a metaphor to tell me to go higher in dimensions or consciousness. I quickly relaxed and fell asleep again.

Soon after falling asleep, I found myself in what seemed to be a dream of some sort. I was standing in an outdoor car park which was about one-hundred feet from where I was sleeping. I found myself gazing into the sky. I had an immense feeling of awe as I stared at one of the most beautiful multi-coloured masses of clouds I had ever seen. I always enjoy the tremendous sense of joy that I get when marvelling at something otherworldly that you could never see in waking life. As I was staring at the clouds, I spotted what could have only been described as a UFO. It was black and was shaped like two spheres connected by a cord, just like in the prior experience. The object was still for a moment, then quickly flew to the left of the entire sky, coming in and out of the clouds dramatically. As it soared, the backside of it let out the most breath-taking sight; floods of enormous multi-coloured clouds trailed from the UFO, filling most of the sky in seconds, like a supervolcano erupting sidewards. The clouds began to pulsate dramatically with giant orbs of colours.

I heard the cracking of thunder, and there was a sudden shift in the atmosphere. An unnerving feeling from the pit of my stomach made me take a step back, but I hit the brick wall of a building behind me, not realising it was there. I scurried into a corner out of an insecure impulse. As the UFO descended, it crashed into the distance and exploded. I ran in the opposite direction. I got out my phone to call a relative in fear that I would die, to tell them I love them, but something in me woke up before doing so. I did the 'hold-nose reality check'. I could breathe through my nose while holding my nostrils shut, making me conscious that I was in a non-physical dimension.

I was thrilled and had to compose myself. I studied my hands in an attempt to attain full waking consciousness. As my mind gained clarity, I witnessed 'subconscious dream projections' dissolve before my eyes; brick walls, tree and fences all began to disappear. After a few moments, my perception was crisp, awake and untainted. I felt that energising non-physical wakefulness that engulfs me every time I have an out of body experience like this. I was on the main road around the corner from where my body was sleeping. The location was an almost perfect replica of the physical version. The only two things that were different were the vast number of people out on the street and an unfamiliar overly-friendly community atmosphere I sensed from them.

The highly positive energy that I felt would suggest that I was in a slightly 'higher-dimensional counterpart' of the physical Earth dimension. The people who were here must have had their consciousness set close to physical Earth consciousness. I considered the possibility that they were people who lived in my town and were asleep, unconsciously projecting. However, that didn't feel right; there was something special and enlightened about this place. Everybody seemed like they were awake and conscious of the fact this was the afterlife. I somehow began to intuit that these were people who had recently died or people who were simply trying to experience life like it was when they were alive. I started to think about parallel worlds and how this is precisely what quantum physicists must be on the verge of discovering. When you experience something like this first-hand, the reality of it hits you profoundly. It's indescribable how tangible it felt and how more natural and joyous it felt than our dense, physical world.

As I walked around, I found myself standing on a pavement with crowds of lively people walking by me. Masses of conversation poured into my ears. I started to walk, but to my surprise, it became a challenge. I had to strain myself into a meditative walk. It was like I was learning to walk for the first time as if I had new legs. I laughed at the thought of what I must have looked like to others. Fortunately, the more I got the hang of it, the stronger I felt. At this point, I felt so alive; I walked along the pavement for a while in pure joy. The atmosphere was positive and enchanted; the sky was dusky and slightly purple. I almost got carried away with the feeling and made a conscious effort to contain myself.

I remembered my intent for out of body experiences; to understand the worlds that exist beyond the physical. I contemplated the lives of the people and observed cheerful friends and families walking past me. I greeted a middle-eastern looking family of five; a mother, father, daughter, son and a grandfather who was in a wheelchair – he instantly threw me into confusion. It was a non-physical world, and he chose to travel around in a wheelchair.

"Do you know that you're dead?" I asked.

They were all grinning. "Yes," they all replied.

"Sorry I was just curious. I'm alive, and I..."

"Yes, we know" they interrupted.

I chuckled in amazement; they were not only conscious of their own death but also somehow knew I lived in the physical world. They continued walking. The son stayed with me for a few minutes and told me about his family. I can't recall most of the conversation; however, I remembered the last part of the conversation.

"Were you all happy to know that you could still spend time together after you died?" I asked.

"Yes," he replied, uninterested as he spotted his family gaining distance.

I noticed then that I was losing feeling on the left side of my face. I felt the numbness of it with my hand. I tried to speak, but to my amazement, I could only utter gibberish. Since I was pretty new to this practice, my strength to remain conscious in this dimension seemed to be coming to its limits. The next thing I know, I was lying in my bed as if there were no break in consciousness.

I reflected in awe at the events that had taken place. I thought about the fact that we could still carry living in an extraordinarily similar afterlife to our physical earthly lives. A part of me had the intuition that the family were purposely with each other to fulfil their wishes of experiencing family-time together that they had missed out on in the physical world. Perhaps because one or more members died unexpectedly, or that because during their lives, other material circumstances stopped them from spending enough time together.

Thus, this is just a glimpse of the type of information and wisdom we can find out in the astral plane, a direct perception of the workings of the afterlife and intimate communication with those who are living out their personal journeys. The afterlife is something we are all barely interested in while alive, but once death comes knocking at the door, it becomes an all-encompassing horizon to discover. Such an experience surely puts into proper perspective all the dramas and events that happened in our life, situations that we took for granted, or things that we got too upset about when we shouldn't have.

BELIEF AND DOUBT

Why is it that many choose not to believe in something that they do not *know* whether to be true or not? Most who decide to hold a belief against non-physical worlds have not experienced it for themselves or have not even tried to experience it. We have to recognise that there is some general consensus amongst conventional wisdom that out of body experiences into the afterlife is something to be sceptical about; otherwise, you would be labelled strange or deluded. But an individual who is interested in finding it out for themselves has to be courageous enough to go against what the many would advise against chasing. In this case, we have to remember what the current state of humanity is in, and that science, which is commonly hailed as the most upright sort of 'proven' truth, is nowhere near understanding the infinite complexity of non-physical reality, science is still very much perplexed at many phenomena in the universe, let alone for them to even begin attempting to understand the non-physical yet.

Today, the 'big bang theory' is still widely accepted as general sound logic, yet it is only a theory, and many don't think about the possibility that what was before the big bang could have been another universe or other non-physical dimension or phenomena that gave birth to ours; such a theory makes sense to an out of body traveller. Physicality is always preceded by non-physicality, with one of the closest layers to the physical dimension being the astral plane. When things are manifested in the physical, it is manifested in the astral first. The astral plane is a sort of foundation to the physical plane.

Suppose we wanted to find the truth behind how the universe came into creation. In that case, we could do so through astral projection. Personally, I think it's logical to assume that material creation is preceded by non-physical mechanisms as its underpinning reality. As many philosophies in the East agree; form cannot exist without the formless, not necessarily the other way around. There has to be nothing in order for there to be something in the same way that space allows planet Earth to be; non-physical dimensions of nature allow physical dimensions to be.

That is a bottomless subject though, but those are my thoughts. You can formulate your own theories after putting in the work for non-physical exploration and make your own mind up. After a while of practising, you will come to your own intuitions about the universe, but let's take it one step at a time; there is no need to stress about such things.

When we see the reality of astral projection for ourselves, our consciousness shifts from a level of 'intellectual speculation' to a level of *knowing*, which goes beyond belief and leaves no room for doubt. From there, one usually gives up overthinking about it again or engaging in debates and instead only wants to continue exploring their newfound state, regardless of other people and their world views.

In the level of consciousness that understands OBEs, nobody can convince you otherwise of its authenticity. You no longer fear sceptics who tell you that astral projection could just be the imagination of your own mind because you instinctively understand the difference between a dream and an authentic experience. One such experience I'd like to share is where I was out of body and confirmed what I saw afterwards with my physical eyes after waking up. I believe many practitioners go through a phase of having such an experience, where they verify what they saw in physical life. I think it usually happens naturally because our subconscious wants to confirm the authenticity of our OBEs for ourselves. Even though it's not necessary, such an experience greatly helps one to solidify their confidence and *knowing* that their experiences are real.

Glowing House: Validating an OBE

7th September 2014

Ever since before I started having astral projection experiences, I never doubted in my mind that the reality of it wasn't objective. This was mainly due to having already practised deep meditation, lucid dreaming, and from reading books on the matter; I was very resolute in my conviction. So when it came to my first time coming out of body directly, my belief turned into deep and self-assured knowledge.

I never looked for proof or confirmation that my experiences were real. I never thought of setting up experiments like other people have done in books I've read, such as getting someone to place a picture or number in another room and then project into there and find out what it is. The direct experience I felt in my heart was proof enough. Nevertheless, one afternoon when taking a midday nap, I found personal proof of OBE phenomena that so many have sought.

It was a sunny summers day, which we don't get much of in the UK. I went for a midday nap and soon found myself coming out of my body. I looked around in amazement as I saw the exact same room and house I was in, but this isn't what astounded me the most; what amazed me was the fact that the air in my house was glowing with a bright and warm golden-yellow light. The house was an exact replica except for just one aspect; this glowing golden light illuminating everything and bringing everything it touched to life, irradiating its splendour in all directions. There were tiny sparkles of white on closer inspection like someone threw fairy dust on everything, like from a Disney movie. It immediately struck me that this must be the wonderful effect that sunlight has on the astral counterparts of our homes.

I walked out of my room and down the corridor enjoying this fantastic glowing version of my house, which felt invigorating and blissful. Once I got to the stairs, I walked halfway down when I noticed my sister sitting on the end of our three-seat sofa in the corner of the living room next to her friend, who I didn't know was visiting. She was on her phone, in her pyjamas, while holding a blue packet of Cheese & Onion Walkers crisps.

On that day, I had been in my room for hours, with no interest or knowledge of where my sister was or what she was doing. Furthermore, we had many different flavours of crisps in the house, and it was the blue packet of crisps that I took note of clearly in my mind. So, I went back to my physical body and woke up; I immediately got up and walked to the stairway, and to my great pleasure, I saw the exact same scene. She was sitting there in the same location, on her phone, in her pyjamas, holding the blue packet of crisps and sitting next to the same friend I saw. I smiled with an inner knowing and satisfaction.

I don't personally feel we need these types of experiences to believe in astral projection. Still, they do certainly help in grounding your self-assurance further. I'm sure experiments similar to this will be carried out more frequently by science in the future, which will play an essential role in influencing more of the masses that astral projection is a plausible prospect.

Even without scientifically recorded evidence, direct experience of the astral itself is often proof enough for most individuals, especially when they examine the astral world closely and realise how genuine it is in their discernment. With the current state of most individuals, I sense that even if a group of scientists proved the reality of astral projection, most people would still be sceptical. It would still ultimately come down to direct experience to truly convince someone.

THE DREAM OF LIFE

The average person wakes up, eats, goes to work, comes back home, sleeps and dreams about the day or some other fantasy. They repeat this cycle till the day they die, with perhaps a handful of lucid moments in-between. What's the purpose of this, and why do we go through life in such a cycle? What if we were to become aware of our dreams, and not only that, but what if we were to stop dreaming altogether? The answer to these questions can be found in the fact that dreaming while awake is no different from when we dream when we sleep. As psychologists notoriously recognise, and what has spilt over into conventional wisdom, is that dreams are usually about the things we did while we were awake. They are simply a reflection of our waking lives. If this is true, one could possibly say it is safe to assume that if you do not dream while awake, then you won't dream while asleep too. In other words, if you are conscious while awake, then you'll be conscious while asleep; this is a core teaching in this book.

What exactly do I mean by 'dreaming while awake'? This is already a challenge for most of us to conceptualise accurately to begin with. Think about the fact that we never know when we are even dreaming when in the dream; therefore, it can be just as difficult, if not more, to understand why we barely ever know that we dream while awake.

When you wake up from a dream, it is easy to admit that "oh

yes, that was definitely a dream, because I was talking to a camel", but what we struggle more to do in waking life is admit the stories we create for ourselves in the physical because we are more identified with them and usually more emotionally attached. Through identification with our ego, we give ourselves reason to stay attached to the dreams we uphold against our reality. People either hold onto worries of the past or anxieties about the future or spend so much time and energy investing in beliefs. On top of this, it is difficult for us to admit that our thoughts about the world hold little reality objectively. Most of our thinking is of little benefit to our lives; in fact, a lot of thinking is the cause of many of our problems. By becoming aware of how and what we think, we understand how to think more effectively and stop thinking when it is not necessary.

"Not to be able to stop thinking is a dreadful affliction, but we don't realise this because almost everyone is suffering from it, so it is considered normal."

- *Eckhart Tolle*

To simplify things further, we could call our entire perception of the world our 'dream of life'. Our dream of life is simply everything we perceive and understand it to be, which includes but is not limited to: concepts, feelings, family, friends, enemies, hobbies, happy moments, sad moments, achievements, likes, dislikes, political dispositions, religious beliefs, scientific beliefs etc. the list goes on; it is the content which we perceive through the television screen of our senses and that we repeat and uphold with our thoughts continually. For example, wherever you are sitting or standing right now, look around you and notice everything you can see, feel, hear, and touch – this is your experience of reality, here and now. Now, the moment you begin to think about any point in the future or any point in the past, you are projecting a part of your consciousness into an imagined dream-reality which ultimately holds no substance for objective reality; our thoughts and dreams about our life do not exist or have objectivity in comparison to direct experience.

Consequently, for most untrained minds, they usually lose most of their awareness from the present moment, due to giving too much focus to the content of their mind; this is a significant obstacle when approaching the art and practice of astral projection, because if we are not going to be aware of and appreciate the present moment in the physical, then how do we expect to do that while out of body when we want to appreciate the present moment of the astral? On top of this, one has to figure out how to move their awareness out of body in the first place; this isn't so easy if the mind is scattered. This is why meditation and prolonged concentration is essential.

So, this is the first step, developing a habit of grounding your awareness in the here and now and not letting yourself excessively daydream. Catch yourself daydreaming throughout the day, and you will most likely catch yourself daydreaming in your dreams at night. The party you will attend next week does not exist yet, and whatever you think about it will only ever be a dream. Everyone attending the party can imagine what it will be like, but the experience will always be different compared to when you actually attend it. In the same way, we imagine what our life should be like and become disappointed in it when it doesn't turn out the way we dreamed of, only furthering our entanglement deeper into the labyrinth of the mind with all its complex emotions, reactions and desires. Similarly, yesterday happened, and you can recall it through memory, but if you carry on analysing yesterday, perhaps you will realise someone was mean to you, and you become offended and upset. Adding this 'personalisation' onto memories of the past is also a form of dreaming that we can become identified with. What has happened in the past has happened, is there really any need to add more content on top of it? What purpose does such thinking have? To delve even more deeply and to talk more frankly – you must realise that this moment, here and now, is all that ever exists; it is the only reality you can rely on because it is the only one you can see and experience directly with your senses.

Suppose you are currently inside a room of your house reading this book. How do you even know that the other rooms in your home exist without actually being there? The truth is, you don't; you only *assume* that it's there. This way of *assuming* everything in our lives is how we come to daydreaming our way into everything, mechanically living through routine on auto-pilot. Every door you open in your house, you unconsciously assume that it's going to be the room you expect; now, when you do this in a dream, you will do the same thing, never questioning whether it's a dream at all and the content of the environment will align perfectly as you always expect it to. But usually, in a dream, even when the environment isn’t what you expect, you still don't question it; this is the deep sleeping state of ordinary human consciousness.

We have to learn to start intensely questioning our reality as a matter of well-trained habit. If there’s anything that ever seems weird or out of the ordinary, we should be automatically asking ourselves whether we’re in a dream or not.

Furthermore, often during our lives, and especially with those who are significantly cut off from reality, we go to meet people already with an idea of them in our heads which isn't actually them. We project those ideas onto them, barely making an effort to truly experience them authentically. This effect can be felt with deeply unconscious people who come across inauthentically. Similarly, we watch famous people on the news and create an idea in our heads about them when they may not necessarily be a reality for us in our personal experience. Yet, many like to think about 'celebrities' often, upholding the existence of mental projections of them as if they are some deity to be worshipped. Daydreaming is literally projecting our awareness into a dream. This is no different from what we do when we're sleeping in bed. Above all of this, we create a dream about ourselves and who we think we are, but what happens when one *thinks* they know who they are? Well, then they never question it; they never ask the question, "Who am I?". Yet this is a profound question that should never leave anyone's curiosity. Such a question serves profound purpose in our lives and it is frankly a tragedy for any individual to not wonder about such things throughout their existence.

You might ask, "But who am I if not what I think about myself?"... is it so difficult to accept that you do not know who you are and that there is personal power to be found in accepting the mysteries of life? The mind always seeks to hungrily know things and is scared of not knowing. Thus, it puts ideas and labels in boxes simply to make us feel comfortable. When we have the courage to drop the ideas and endless identifications about ourselves, only then does the reality about ourselves start to emerge.

"I have no routines or personal history. One day I found out that they were no longer necessary for me and, like drinking, I dropped them. One must have the desire to drop them and then one must proceed harmoniously to chop them off, little by little. If you have no personal history, no explanations are needed; nobody is angry or disillusioned with your acts. And above all, no one pins you down with their thoughts. It is best to erase all personal history because that makes us free from the encumbering thoughts of other people. I have, little by little, created a fog around me and my life. And now nobody knows for sure who I am or what I do. Not even I. How can I know who I am, when I am all this?"

- *Don Juan Matus (Carlos Castaneda)*

When you understand the implications of excessive personal identifications with worldly things and rid yourself of all the useless dreams you give your energy to, you start to learn to individualise your own consciousness and gain more power over what kind of reality or what kind of 'dream of life' you want to consciously create; that's right, I'm not saying that dreaming is an inherently bad thing, it is a creative gift from nature, the main issue is that we don't understand how to use this gift. We use it unconsciously and destructively; just look at the state of humanity and its obsession with negative thinking. Thus, this is also one of the first steps to everything spoken about in this book; realising that you are always dreaming, even when 'awake'. Moreover, through this realisation, you begin to have more control over whether you want to 'dream' at all. If you've ever wondered about the meaning of grace, this is it. By stopping dreaming and surrendering to the flow of life, you'll realise that you never needed to control anything in your life in the first place, and everything happens naturally as it does anyway.

"True initiates do not dream. Dreams are for those who are asleep. True initiates live in the higher worlds, out of the physical body, in a state of intensified wakefulness without ever dreaming."

- *Samael Aun Weor*

You may think, "But I'm not thinking of anything right now? I'm not dreaming?", the fact is, we hold so many beliefs, thoughts and identifications within us that there is far more going on in the mind than we usually realise on the surface, this can boil down also to the way we feel about everything; one's 'vibration' so to speak. Our dreams have become habituations that have fallen into the abyss of subconscious and unconscious ways of being.

There are infinite levels of inner stillness and quietude of the mind. In the profound experience of meditation, one can start to witness the hallucinations that appear when awareness becomes tranquil and disidentified enough to notice them. There are deep layers to our consciousness, and every thought, belief, and identification that we hold within us determines how we are, what we feel, how we speak and how we perceive. It's how we are vibrationally or energetically. When is the last time you checked in with yourself and took a good look at what you were thinking or felt how you were really *feeling*? This is another great habit to ask yourself throughout the day. You can ask yourself at any time during waking life, "What am I thinking?" and "What am I feeling?". Don't respond to yourself mechanically. Simply be silent and observe; awareness is all that is needed.

When is the last time you really looked around your surroundings and became present without thought? When is the last time you appreciated the things around you? If you can remember when you last did that, consider how long you did it for and whether you even valued those moments of presence. These moments of being in the present moment, which should be our natural state, are not frequent enough. Thus, we become lost and trapped inside the imaginings and endless chatter in the skull. We get caught up in what others say and in the world around us, reacting to everything we see and offering a personal opinion on any matter. We create stories in our head about our happy or sad past, the problems we have in our present circumstances, and possible difficulties or fortunes you may or may not come into in the future. But consider, for one moment, of letting go of all of this. Do you not feel more liberated and freer in doing so?

I am emphasising these points at length because these states of consciousness are synonymous with our dreams, which are absolutely responsive to our inner state. Therefore, such states can completely determine whether you will project yourself into a dream or into an objective reality when you sleep at night.

If you are in a dream, what you think can often manifest precisely the way you want instantly, if you have trained yourself well. However, in the astral, the environment is slightly different, objects don't manifest exactly according to what you're thinking; it is, however, more responsive to how you're *feeling*, and if you are a very anxious or fearful person, it could be more likely that you will go to lower and darker regions of the astral plane because that is more matched with your state of consciousness. Similarly, suppose one is a highly positive and happy person. In that case, they are more likely to end up in more pleasant and sublime realms.

The average person lives in a perpetual dream-like state throughout their entire lives, not stopping for a single moment to consider whether the content of their lives is even a dream at all. The benefits of becoming conscious of our dreams are far-reaching, from realising how to achieve our goals in life, improving our relationships, and of course, having mind-expanding out-of-body experiences beyond the physical and attaining spiritual enlightenment.

At this point, you might wonder why I'm talking so in-depth about the awakening of consciousness and how it all relates to astral projection. Frankly, these points are not emphasised enough in most books on astral projection. Astral projection is a spiritual practice in its essence, after all, not some inconsequential fantasy. Spiritual balance and well-being are all synonymous with it, and all help build a foundation in understanding the mysteries behind perception and OBEs. Travelling out of the body is an awakening in and of itself. It is profoundly beneficial to understand what is really going on to appreciate it for what it is when it happens. We have to value this experience, just as we choose to love superficial things like celebrities, sports or money.

If you want to learn how to astral project, you need to put in the work. You need to study the subject, read, watch videos, get inspired, meditate and practice. Some are more natural at this than others, but regardless, anyone can do it; you need only to make an effort to master it like with anything in life. Practice makes perfect. It's the same as learning martial arts; you have to get up, go to the dojo, get to know the techniques, how it feels, and align them with your body and mind until mastered.

Through practical understanding alone, we get rid of the need for ineffective methods and complex practices that harbour self-doubt, often seen in books that promise quick results through techniques backed by little explanation. When we instinctively comprehend the mechanics behind out of body experiences, we adopt our own intuitive practice.

This book should provide new thought-provoking contemplation for you to ponder even when you finish a reading session, like food for the soul. Yes, I've said that thinking *can* be useless, but attaining profound and continuous no-thought states of bliss while awake and asleep, is not something acquired in a day. It takes work and a firm resolve to live a better and more spiritually enriching life. This starts with feeding your mind with better content and more critical thinking.

Accordingly, when we speak of out of body experiences, we are not talking about some separate or man-made experience; we are dealing with life itself, not some strange phenomena that only a few experience. It is inherent to all of us, but most of us just aren't conscious of it. This is why we have to address our lives, and not just astral projection as a sort of separate hobby or casual interest. It is a wholesome practise that affects us positively and profoundly on every level of our *Being*. Observe any Kung Fu Master; he does not just partake in his martial art every now and then for fun, no. He takes it seriously, and he lives his life through the philosophy his martial art teaches just as much as when he is fighting. He grows and builds his character as a result. The path of astral projection is absolutely the same, if not more. One has to truly look at oneself; it takes strength and courage to be honest and let go of certain aspects of ourselves. Attachment is a real thing. This is the way of the spiritual warrior.

"A warrior acknowledges his pain but he doesn't indulge in it. The mood of the warrior who enters into the unknown is not one of sadness; on the contrary, he's joyful because he feels humbled by his great fortune, confident that his spirit is impeccable, and above all, fully aware of his efficiency. A warrior's joyfulness comes from having accepted his fate, and from having truthfully assessed what lies ahead of him."

- *Don Juan Matus (Carlos Castaneda)*

You may be disappointed to find that I don't put primary emphasis on some all-promising ultimate step-by-step method. There are reasons for this, which has to do with the very reason why so many attempt to come out of body but fail. From a young age, our minds have been conditioned to solve problems and carry out tasks by methodological approaches. This is great for mundane tasks, but when it comes to the transcendental and liberating experience of astral travel, we also need to transcend methods; more specifically, we need to transcend thinking. We rely too much on and seek step-by-step manuals for consciousness as if it's a microwave meal. The reality is that the intelligence of consciousness is beyond intellectual comprehension. What a mistake it is to assume that the mind has control over consciousness or that it can understand it through labels and language; the opposite is true; consciousness is *always* in control of the mind whether we have a false sense of it or not. It is in the very depths of transcendental consciousness that all spiritual truths are discovered.

Journey into these dimensions of presence and lucidity while you're awake, and you'll journey into them while you're sleeping. I will, of course, provide various practices throughout the book and reveal a sort of summarised version of my personal approach. With that said, I hope by the time you read this book, you understand that astral projection is more effective when we approach it intuitively and instinctively through the heart's intelligence. Although you may think that's a vague way to describe it, it's absolutely true in practice. The centre of the heart is far more superior in knowing how to astral project than the brain.

I want to make this clear; this book will never be the root cause that enables you to astral project; no book can do that. Ultimately, you will only ever do it for yourself; I only hope that in conveying my understanding of these realities, it will help you to intuit the practice for yourself.

Another thing that should be absolutely clear is that these non-physical realities, that modern science knows so little about, are accessible to us all directly, no matter who you are, your age, and what you believe in. You can come from any religion and any belief system. Some belief systems may make it more difficult than others, but this has absolutely nothing to do with whether you are a scientist, a religious person, or anywhere in-between.

In fact, a scientist can have more chance of astral travelling than a religious person and vice versa depending on their kinds of belief. For example, some distinguished scientists are more inclined to objective states of consciousness. They will restrain from believing in anything until they openly experiment with it for themselves. On the other hand, a highly religious person may think that astral projection is some sort of sin; to this, I say, how can something so natural to our *Being* ever be a sin? It is as natural as learning to breathe more consciously. Such a belief can get in the way of your attempts. On the other hand, a scientist who holds a belief that there is nothing more to reality other than what we can see physically could have a more challenging time having an out of body experience. On the other hand, a religious person who prays to every type of God and asks them to bring them out of their body to experience heavenly planes of existence would probably have a much greater chance of doing so. At the end of the day, it's all about keeping an open mind, no matter what your background or beliefs are.

You see, taking up the art and practice of astral projection is not learning something new or creating a new skill. You are simply becoming aware of an innate ability that resides as part of your consciousness already. It is not some 'weird' or a 'god-like' power; it is entirely normal and ordinary. In the same way that many aspire to know themselves more deeply, astral projection is just another aspect of that. *Know Thyself.*

Exercise 1: Centering Consciousness

1. Take a deep breath and inhale relaxation into your belly, and exhale with feelings of peace and surrender, repeat as many times as you enjoy. While doing this, become the observer of your breath. Then allow the breath to continue in its automatic natural cycle, but maintain your watching awareness of it. Notice how it naturally goes in and out without any conscious effort.
2. Ask yourself, "How am I feeling?". Expand your awareness to your body, especially your heart area, while keeping a soft focus on your breath. Do not answer the question mentally; only breathe and *feel*.
3. Ask yourself, "What am I thinking?". Do not go too deeply or forcefully into your thoughts. Stay in impartial, objective, non-judging awareness.
4. Continue to breathe while having this newfound state of awareness of your breath, emotions and thoughts.
5. Look around you slowly, without labelling things or

focusing on specific objects; simply take in the visual experience as a whole, like a baby would.

6. Do the same with sounds, don't listen to any particular sound, but listen to the 'soundtrack' of life as a whole, so to speak—neutral and detached.
7. Exercise appreciation of your experience, it could be anything; the beauty of sunlight coming in through a window, flowers, or simply the fact that you are alive and experiencing the wonderful and mystical experience that is life, which is enriching to perceive when you no longer label things or narrate a story over them.
8. Try to maintain this no-thought state of appreciation and centeredness by staying with the breath and a soft feeling in your heart area. If you can hold this throughout your day, you will make vast improvements to your health, quality of life and astral projection practice.

If you follow these steps mindfully and intuitively, you may find yourself submerging into a deep state; close your eyes and explore it. Allow yourself to go more deeply into it without thinking, but remember to stay present and not steer off course into random dreams.

You can this formally as a meditation without moving, for a set amount of time once or twice a day. You can set a timer for ten or fifteen minutes and see how long you can maintain general focus and presence without being interrupted by unwanted thoughts and emotions. After some practice, you can extend the amount of time to thirty minutes or even an hour. Suppose you do this before bed for an extended period. In that case, I almost guarantee you will notice exciting improvements in your dreams' vividness and content, assuming you have trained yourself to remember your dreams by writing them in a journal every morning.

WE COME OUT OF BODY EVERY NIGHT

Something that you'll rarely see discussed amongst astral projection books is the fact that you actually come out of body every night unconsciously.

In the field of both modern and traditional medicine, cultures from around the world all recognise that certain behaviours and psychological characteristics affect our health. For example, there are numerous spiritual and scientific studies to suggest that the emotion of anger can have a damaging effect on specific organs, and I think there is a growing consensus among the collective on this. The physical body is under constant stress, not so much from external sources, but from our own psychological state, especially in our reactions towards external reality, whatever it may be. Therefore, when the body sleeps, this part of our consciousness, our psychological state, needs to leave the physical body so that it can allow the body to heal itself naturally, without the 'disturbances' of the ego affecting it, and enter many hours of much-needed rest and deep breathing. It's only when we enter back into our bodies when we wake up that we begin our compulsive thinking again for the day and forget to consciously breathe; notice how your own and others' breathing can be very shallow while awake but very deep when asleep, this is especially true for those who are more cut off from their *Being*.

You may also notice spontaneous sudden physical 'jerks' as you fall to sleep sometimes and are abruptly woken up by it. This 'jerk' is actually your astral body, or consciousness, falling, or 'snapping', back to your physical body as you oscillate towards the realm of sleep.

The Difference Between Lucid Dreaming & Astral Projection

Accordingly, when we sleep at night, consciousness leaves the body and enters the world of dreams. In this sense, you can call dreaming a sort of unconscious form of astral projection.

If you go outside and look at a crowd of people who are all in the same physical location; in reality, they are actually all in a world, or dream of their own, in their heads, so to speak. This is much like what it is like in the astral plane too, when consciousness roams out of the body at night it's often not in the objective astral experience that it should be, but more in a subjective dream world of our own imagination.

At first, it may not seem that there is a lot of difference between lucid dreaming and astral projection. Still, one of the keys to identifying it is in how the experience feels. For beginners, you shouldn't stress about this difference too much. Both phenomena are non-physical realities, and both have much significance and learning opportunities for you. Dreams can be vivid, yes, but there is a distinct hyper-realism and 'knowing' to astral projection, especially when you feel yourself coming out of your body and standing in your room.

In their deepest essence, though, lucid dreaming and astral projection are very different. One description you can say is that dreams are an inward subjective experience of your own creation of infinite possibilities, but that astral projection is an outward objective experience of actual dimensions that have laws and limitations similar to the physical plane. Unlike dreams, the astral plane is a natural and tangible place where you can interact with others. Sometimes there are experiences blurred between the astral and dreams, and it can be difficult to tell the difference. There's no absolute formula to know whether it's a dream or the astral unless you are experienced, which usually comes after years of practice and consistency in discerning them. What's important, though, is that we learn from wherever we find ourselves in the non-physical; dreams can be just as, if not more significant and profound than astral projection, in terms of learning about one's spiritual progress. Many people who seek the experience of astral projection overlook the experience of dreams, but this is a beginner's mistake. Dreams are essential; they reveal the things we need to work on the most - things we need to move past; because if you want to astral project, you need to stop dreaming and be present in reality, free from fantasies and compulsive thoughts; especially destructive ones. These are often revealed to us in our dreams at night. They can be hidden through metaphorical and symbolic meanings, and you can purchase 'dream dictionary' books for this, but the best way to interpret them is through practice, introspection and intuition.

When you understand that we come out of body every night, it can answer many questions for your own practice. For example, many people often stress about what 'special' things they should do while going to sleep in order to come out of body, such as what position they should sleep in, but in reality, all that is required is normal relaxing sleep! You may either become conscious during the 'falling to sleep' phase and become aware of the separation that occurs during this time, or you will spontaneously become conscious during the middle of an unconscious out of body experience or dream that is happening already. The key is in setting intention to become aware before sleeping: as you drift off, you can affirm to yourself, "I will become conscious during sleep".

I've had numerous encounters with people on the astral plane where I immediately know that they are not conscious that they are out of body. One particularly significant and eventful experience is where around a hundred people were supposedly unaware of being out of body, who were all attending a 'class'.

A Priestess's Teaching on the Ego

23rd January 2021

I begin in a dream. I am in my uncle's house, it's night time, and we're getting ready for bed. My uncle is setting up a bed for me in his conservatory, to which there is a beautiful open field with moonlight across its expanse; I mention how the energy here is perfect for astral projection. He asks me about the subject, and we discuss it for a couple of minutes. After, I go to bed and fall asleep within the dream peacefully. Next, I find myself walking across the field near where I just went to sleep and realise that it's a dream. I had been reading about shapeshifting in a book on shamanism by Merilyn Tunneshende recently, and I attempted one of her methods for it. I decide to turn into a black panther. I went on all four limbs and walked in the form of a large cat for a few minutes. Afterwards, I decide to go beyond the dream and enter the astral. I counted down slowly from five to one with the intention of carefully moving my awareness back to my physical body, and then coming out of it again.

As expected, I felt myself become aware of my physical body; however, the transition from the dream to the physical was slow enough that I easily avoided moving or fully occupying any part of my physical body. Instead, I immediately floated upwards out of my body, and flew directly out on the street in front of my apartment. It was the morning time, and since I was living in London city centre at the time, I saw and felt the hustle and bustle of morning city life. It was busy with cars and people. This made me feel a bit unbalanced, and so I sat on the pavement floor cross-legged and meditated and focused on some breathing. I kept my eyes open so that I stayed grounded in this astral counterpart of the physical. As I meditated, my awareness amplified tenfold. I noticed the detail of the pavement, the blue sky and early morning rays and the beautiful rustling of the lush trees on the roads, which are so prominent in London. I got a few strange looks from strangers; I couldn't tell whether the people I looked at were in the physical or astral. I analysed the cream-coloured cement pavement floor and the black iron fences which were next to me. I felt hyperrealism come over me. I touched the cold, roughly black painted fence bars; they felt as physical as they were in waking life, if not more. I walked down the street for a bit after this. Then, I looked over at a familiar church near where I lived; it looked the same as it did in the physical. However, opposite this church, there is usually a roundabout which has a park in the middle of it. But, in this astral counterpart of the location, instead of an empty park, I saw a huge temple, cleaner and more majestic than the usual physical church across the road! I made my way over.

I walked up about fifteen steps to this huge wooden doorway. I opened it slightly and peeked inside; I was surprised to see around one hundred people attending what I thought was a religious mass. Intrigued, I quietly walked in and sat down on the back row. Everyone was sat quietly listening. To my surprise, I was delighted to see a woman, a priestess giving a sermon. On the platform, it was just her, sitting casually on a humble chair behind a standard table. I soon realised that this was far from a traditional religious mass that we usually see in churches in the physical, but a class, or teaching from a wise 'astral helper', and actually I recognised her as a spiritual master according to what my Gnostic teacher had taught me about them; that spiritual masters in the astral plane can be identified by the colour of the robes many of them wear – white and silver; this is what the priestess was wearing. She looked at me smiling while she talked, I smiled back. I thought she was quite generous doing this, considering the number of people here attending. But during this eye contact, I soon realised she was multitasking; she was telepathically communicating to me while also answering questions from people at the same time. This must take some real skill. She said to me, "I recognise you, enjoy the experience, but you don't have to stay; this is for the public. These are basic teachings." I acknowledged this telepathic communication, and I continued to stay anyway, fascinated by the whole situation. I looked at all the people, and I got a strong intuition that most here were unconsciously projecting out of their bodies. Almost everyone seemed overly excited and fascinated, but not in a controlled way, affirming my perception that they were not fully aware, in the total sense of the word. One person asked a question relating to God. To answer it, the priestess directed everyone to turn to the Quran and the Bible and discuss it. What a beautiful event to witness, people studying texts from different traditions, compared to usual meetings in churches. After the priestess finished explaining a verse in the Quran, she asked everyone to get out their handmade 'masks', which she had previously asked them to make. I look around in wonder at everyone's tattered handcrafted wooden masks.

They looked like shamanic masks, all charming and imperfectly unique, made out of dark wood. It was clear to me that this was a symbolic lesson on the ego. Everyone started showing each other their masks, proud of what they had made. Shortly after, the priestess went around, one by one taking peoples' masks and inspecting them. She used a 'magic' pen to tap on each mask and turned them into splendorous gold, fixing all their imperfections. The priestess goes to one woman to take her mask, but the woman is upset and distressed and says, "I don't want my masks turning into gold", the priestess calmly takes the mask from her anyway and says emphatically, "This is necessary". She turns the mask into gold and gives it back. The woman seems stunned and just stares at her mask. The previously excited atmosphere had mysteriously shifted now; there was a silence as everyone looked on in awe. There appeared to be a shift in the atmosphere. On a deep subconscious level, there seemed to be learning and information being communicated through this act of the mask changing to gold compared to when they were just discussing things about the Quran and the Bible.

As the priestess continued to go to each person, she eventually came to me; I didn't have a mask. Instead, she smiled and kindly held my wrist, revealing a bracelet with a crucifix pendant hanging from it. She turned the pendant into gold. I told her thank you and smiled. After some time, a new person comes through the door, and I'm surprised to see it's someone I know; a colleague from an old workplace. She was often in a sad or hurt mood in physical life, I was curious to see her here. She shouted happily, "Wow, this is amazing! Thank you, I'm so excited to be here!", everyone claps and responds with happiness. The priestess welcomes her and calms her down and says in a sombre mood, "Yes, but you must wait, the path isn't easy, and we have to suffer; you have to accept and work through your suffering."

A significant thing I learned from this experience was that the way we are influenced at night is not by intellectual learning but by things that make a powerful impression on our consciousness. This is how influential OBEs can be on our subconscious at night and why it can be of great spiritual significance to become aware of what is happening in our sleep. I believe many of us unconsciously attend these sorts of classes during sleep more often than we realise.

One thing I found peculiar, and how I could tell everyone was dreaming, was by how overly happy and fascinated everyone seemed; similar to how people become too engrossed with what they see while watching TV, I could see their unconsciousness in their eyes. Furthermore, what I noticed is what happens to many on the spiritual path; people reach out to spiritual teachings out of sadness in the hope of attaining happiness, but once they find a tiny grain of wisdom that brings them joy, perhaps thinking they have found enlightenment, then they are content for a small amount of time and continue their life as usual until they become depressed again. Not realising that the tiny drop of wisdom they found was only a minuscule part of an entire ocean of spiritual happiness and knowledge. Hence, this is the state of humanity, chasing any opportunity for happiness and running away with it, not genuinely honouring it and comprehending it, nor making an effort to remember it. It's important to remember that whenever we make efforts on the spiritual path, no matter what sort of realisations we come to, there will always be deeper aspects and levels of consciousness for us to comprehend.

"Whatever plane our consciousness may be acting in, both we and the things belonging to that plane are, for the time being, our only realities. As we rise in the scale of development, we perceive that during the stages through which we have passed, we mistook shadows for realities, and the upward progress of the Ego is a series of progressive awakenings, each advance bringing with it the idea that now, at last, we have reached 'reality'; but only when we shall have reached the absolute Consciousness, and blended our own with it, shall we be free from the delusions produced by Maya (illusion)."

- *Helena Blavatsky*

DREAMING

As you are probably sensing by now, my message is a direct one: a call for people to wake up out of the dream of life and really look within. Perhaps if we were in another era, I would describe the awakening of consciousness more indirectly and perhaps more scientifically and academically, dabbling in and out of scientific books and referencing them trying to convince you of this reality like a university thesis, but I genuinely believe, considering the current state of humanity, that this information needs to be passionately and personably expressed to the world more than ever. There is so much suffering in these times, and many people are increasingly becoming entangled deeper in their minds more than ever. On the other hand, amongst all this, there is an immense opportunity for spiritual realisation amongst all the chaos and spiritual darkness of the twenty-first century. Consciousness can only take so much suffering and illusion until the dam breaks, and an influx of peering beyond the dream of life appears. The ideas in this book are becoming more prevalent in collective consciousness more and more every year, with even younger generations taking an interest.

Out of body realisation can have profound implications on the consciousness of an individual. The process of leaving the body is an awakening in and of itself, an awakening to that which exists beyond physical reality and imagination, beyond delusion. Some may become so shocked at the experience that they may question whether the out of body experience was, in fact, a hallucination, but it's simply not the case if one does not over scrutinise. It is an experience where one realises and connects the dots between *all* religions and spiritual traditions. It is a unified field of awareness which any living being can access. It is my sincere hope that these phenomena be explored more in-depth by modern science, but more importantly by individuals around the world, and that this subject is not seen as strange, supernatural or fiction, but that it is accepted as a natural and regular occurrence that we all can have, just like dreams, but on an infinitely more profound level.

It is first important to understand what actually is the dream state and how it can be a gateway, but also a barrier to having out of body experiences. As we grow up as children, we learn how to understand language and interpret the world intellectually. Our parents and schools reinforce the importance of focusing on our future; thus, this is one place where dreaming begins. We begin to imagine and fantasise about what our future might be in all of its infinite possible timelines. As we grow into our teenage lives, we become more self-aware, and the future doesn't just dwell on our minds, but now the image of ourselves and our egoic makeup dwells on us too; thus, we deliberate not just on the future, but on present circumstances too; on how we look, our opinions, social status, friends etc. Thus, we choose our egos and form them unconsciously.

The emphasis on childhood here is always on the future. Then after focusing on the future for so long, we reach middle age and begin to form doubts and regrets about the decisions we made in our lives. Consequently, we begin to have our focus on the past now too. Regardless, what is important to notice is that the entire time, as we imagine our past, present or future, we are needlessly imagining and visualising in our minds. That which we imagine is not direct reality - but as we imagine, our mind and subconscious doesn't usually know what's reality or not and reacts accordingly. Thus, our lives become a perpetual dream while we're awake and also while we sleep. This dream state we live in the waking life spills into our sleep at night. One can simply drop these dream states and improve their chances of coming out of body, through giving up on dreaming.

Additionally, another reason why there's such gravitation towards these dreams and ideas about ourselves and our lives is identity. There is an inherent need in our souls to feel we belong somewhere, and it derives from our divinity, our core essence, that is deep within. However, since most people don't think about or understand what this essence or consciousness is, it is projected instead towards all sorts of things to identify with; whether it's as part of a country, group, family, job, sexuality, gender, diet, hobby etc. Almost everyone finds something to identify with, and if it's not anything listed above, then the identification can be towards something that happened in life, such as 'being a wife who divorced', 'a man who lost his business' or 'someone who grew up in poverty', the mind always seeks to find identification with life situations to enforce a false self of sense. Yet, this sense of self is not genuine; it is not who you are. Who you are is consciousness, awareness, untainted from these 'dream-projections'. You are that silent presence here and now reading this book; it has no identity, no judgement, no personal issues, it is simply you, yet it is also everything that *is*. Such ego-based identifications can be hard to acknowledge and accept, never mind even going beyond them. With that said, the truth is, as long as you accept and recognise them for what they are without judgement, you can let go of being attached to them naturally. All that is needed is awareness, just in the same way that shining a torch into darkness makes darkness no longer exist. Through shining the light of awareness into the darkness of the unconscious, we naturally begin to transcend unwanted layers of ourselves.

There is a famous saying deriving from Hermeticism, which has been incredibly influential amongst occult and esoteric topics, which is; "As Above, So Below" – we can understand this by saying that what happens on one level of reality also occurs in one form or another on every other level; the microcosm and the macrocosm behave alike, in a relationship. For example, what we dream in the day, we dream at night.

It's clear that we need to stop thinking in order to stop dreaming, but it's also important to be gentle and careful and not too hard on ourselves. It is natural for our consciousness to dream and imagine; we are just too used to abusing these faculties and don't use them effectively. The best way we can learn to use the mind effectively is to give ourselves a break and stop using it altogether for a while, and in doing so, recognise the benefits. One benefit being that when one realises that they are dreaming in waking life, they have taken the first step to awaken.

"Dream Yoga teaches how to take advantage of the dream state and utilise it for our spiritual advancement. Although interest in this subject is growing, there are many people who have been frustrated in their attempts to have their own personal experience of the Astral Worlds. Reading books or attending seminars usually leaves the seeker with more questions, doubts, and contradictions. We have given many clues in order to consciously travel with the Astral Body, so thousands of students have learned to travel in their Astral Body. However, we have seen in practice that those people who cannot quiet the mind, not even for an instant, who are accustomed to hopping from school to school, from book to book, always inquiring, always preoccupied, struggle more to consciously Astral travel. The key is in effort and practice. This starts with the awakening of your consciousness here and now, in the physical world, from moment to moment. To awaken consciousness, we must stop dreaming, and this must be in each moment. When we are in the physical world, we must learn to be awake from moment to moment. We then live awakened and self-conscious from moment to moment in the Astral Worlds, both during the hours of the sleep of the physical body and also after death."

- *Samael Aun Weor*

LUCID DREAMING AS A PREREQUISITE TO ASTRAL PROJECTION

I've noticed many people who wish to astral project go straight into it without learning about helpful tools commonly taught in lucid dreaming resources. It's certainly possible to learn astral projection without it, but if you're struggling, it's completely logical to learn some lucid dreaming basics. I've personally never stopped basic practices of lucid dreaming, such as using reality checks. Ever since before I knew astral projection was even a thing, I had hundreds of lucid dreams beforehand, which no doubt helped me in the future, especially in recognising the difference between these two phenomena.

Dreams are a natural gateway to the non-physical, and since we are all accustomed to at least remembering a few dreams, it is a great place to start. The problem is that we commonly overlook and underestimate the significance of dreams amongst conventional knowledge, subjecting these spiritually relevant experiences to simply 'unimportant fantasies of the mind'. The truth is, dreams are highly important, and yes, even though they are ultimately illusions, these illusions have a tangible reality within your own microcosm, your own inner world, and the information presented to you in dreams is of absolute significance to your own personal and spiritual growth. For example, if you have violent dreams, then it may be a sign you need to work on anger, or if you're always crying in dreams, then there may be some emotions you need to work through. Similarly, recurring dreams are usually a sign that there's something you've not accepted or are struggling to come to terms with. All such things are keeping us locked in the level of dreams as opposed to experiencing the astral plane.

Most ordinary people are disconnected from their *Being* because they're too concerned with worldly matters, dramas and preoccupations. Accordingly, dreams show us what we need to look at the most, the things we need to become conscious of and integrate psychologically so that we may move deeper into more profound levels of our own psyche. For example, suppose you find yourself in a dream that you cannot snap out of or even control. In that case, you are inside a subconscious experience that is so powerful that your subconscious basically forces you to look at it and experience it. If you are lucid in this situation, it is better to go along with the dream and see what you can learn rather than trying to control it. You can ask the scene and characters questions about what they mean; they will usually reply with or do something thought-provoking or insightful.

Dreams can also be an indicator of where we are or what we're currently going through on our spiritual path. For example, those who start meditating and working on themselves and want to astral project often start finding that they have dreams of dying or death. This is often symbolic of the fact that we are 'psychologically' dying. In other words, egoic aspects of ourselves are 'dying', which of course, is a good thing and a sign of overcoming old behavioural patterns. It means we are transcending ourselves. If we transcend ourselves, we go beyond our illusions of the world and get closer to more objective perceptions of physical and non-physical reality.

To analyse different experiences, we begin to have at night, we have to think more intelligently beyond the concepts of *only* lucid dreams and *only* astral projections. In reality, there are various degrees on the spectrum of lucidity and awareness. We could vaguely describe them as:

1. Fully unconscious.
2. Unconscious vivid.
3. Slightly aware but still unconscious decision-making.
4. Aware of the dream but only slight control.
5. Aware of the dream with some control over decision-making but without a full sense of self.
6. Fully lucid with complete control over decisions and remembering of oneself.
7. Letting go of and collapsing the dream state altogether and entering the astral plane.

Accordingly, awareness can become so great that it can go beyond the dream state and enter astral projection. As awareness grows in non-physical space, you begin to awaken out of the dream and into an objective non-physical reality. This is the most natural way to astral project from a lucid dream - through inner realisation that you are in fact the dreamer of the dream, and as a result; you can innately feel the capacity to let go of the dream. See the following diagram:

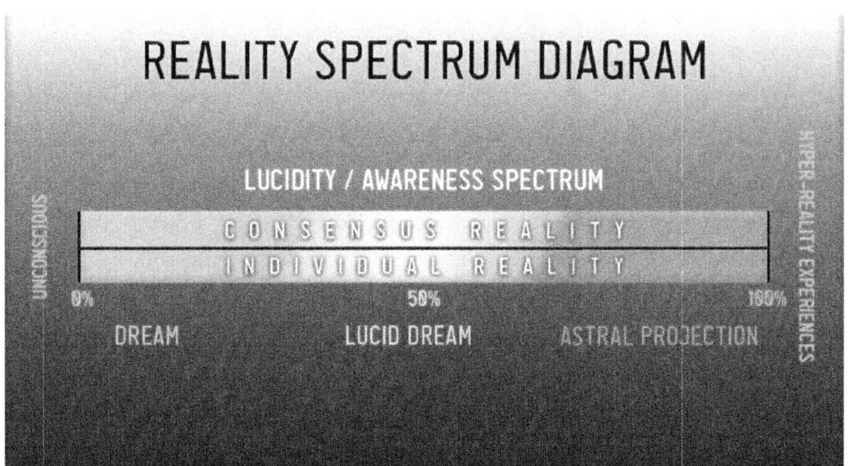

This diagram represents the relationship between how levels of our awareness correspond to our dreams, lucid dreams and the astral plane. See the scale of how a dream is traditionally linked to being unconscious. As you look towards the right, awareness grows into a lucid dream and, eventually, into astral projection. On a more profound aspect, we also have 'Individual Reality' and 'Consensus Reality', which can apply to all three states of awareness displayed in the diagram. Individual reality means an experience where only you are in the environment.

In contrast, consensus reality is typically an environment that you can share with others. This diagram was created by a Reddit user called u/XI_Vanquish_IX, and he explains:

> "Traditionally, we would call all dreams individual experiences. However, in the realm of astral projection discussions, dreams are often associated with experiences of low or lower lucidity/awareness, and the truth is many of these experiences are not individual realities. It is also possible to have individual experiences of astral projection."

This is the complexity of non-physical phenomena. Dreams *can* be in the astral plane, and astral projection can also be in 'private space' such as when one starts to remember past lives. Many other astral projectors also give descriptions of 'unconsciously shared dreams', and there are accounts of friends who have exactly the same dream by 'coincidence'. Similarly, take a look at the following diagram I made to give a crude idea of where levels of reality belong in relation to different levels of perception and non-physical experiences, along with key-words to provide a generalised idea of each one:

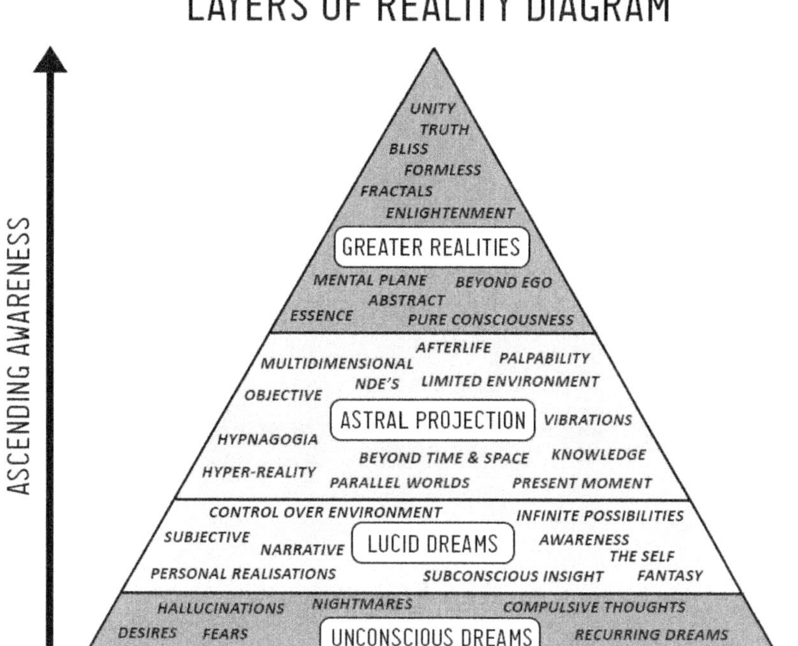

Each keyword is not limited to each section on the pyramid - they can, of course, exist in different parts, but these are generally the most common way to place them. Additionally, 'Greater Realities' reflects the dimensions in non-physical nature that are beyond the astral; for the astral is only one layer of reality. The astral is one of the dimensions most closely linked and similar to the physical, making it easier and more familiar to recognise and talk about. However, the dimensions which exist beyond the astral are so profound, so formless, that talking about such realities only do them less justice. 'Greater Realities' are to do with when we reach a level of consciousness that transcends the astral; these are commonly known as the sixth and seventh dimension and higher, also known as the 'Mental Plane' and 'Causal Plane'.

REALITY CHECKS: A DEEPER LOOK

One thing that dreams and astral projection have in common is that they are both non-physical experiences; reality checks involve using this to our advantage in order to effectively discern whether we're in a non-physical environment unconsciously or not. A reality check is a new habit we form where we ask ourselves at least six or more times a day whether we're dreaming, and we confirm this with a reality check. The more we do this in daily life, the more chances we have of doing it as a habit in our dreams. This is highly effective if you form the habit correctly. You see, most of this work, whether it be lucid dreaming or astral projection, is actually a matter of communicating with our subconscious and getting it to work in our favour. This is an excellent example of relying on our subconscious to give us spontaneous experiences throughout our nights. A few of my favourite reality checks are:

- Use your fingertips to hold your nostrils shut and see if you can breathe through them. If you can't, you're in the physical; if you can, then you're in the non-physical.
- Jump to see if you can fly; if you can, you're in the non-physical; if you can't then, you're in physical life.
- Pull one of your fingers to try and extend it to make it longer; if you can't, then you're in the physical. If you can, then you're in a non-physical environment.

The crucial part here is to really consider you are unconsciously dreaming or in the astral plane. When you perform a reality check, you must expect that you WILL, in fact, breathe through your nostrils, extend a finger, or fly in the sky! Have no doubt in your mind. If you don't do it intensely in this spirit, you can easily perform a reality check in a dream, and it won't work. For example, you may try to fly in a dream but drop back down to the ground simply through unconscious expectation and assumption. If this happens, you're performing reality checks wrong, and you're expecting to drop back down as you do in daily life without really believing you could actually be in a dream. Do the reality check again with more vigour and deliberation! Stop assuming your experience is always in the physical world!

In dreams, many absurd things happen; you could be having a conversation with a camel and not question it. It's only when we wake up do we think it was strange. So, in the same way in our daily lives, we must honestly consider the possibility that we could actually be dreaming, no matter how ordinary things seem. Look around your room now. Are you dreaming? How do you know you're not? Unless you're Buddha or some spiritual master, you don't know, and one of the only ways for you to accurately confirm this is with a reality check.

Cultivating Reality-Checking Awareness

Another sort of reality check is a more active one that we can develop in our everyday perception of the world, which I call 'reality-checking awareness'. This can be done by 'looking around corners' or 'opening doors', or looking anywhere really. The greatness of this method is that it's effective even if you're at home all day and nothing unusual is happening. Others won't even notice what you're doing. To do this, whenever you walk around a corner of your house, take a moment in your mind to recall what *should* be around the corner, remember what it should look like, note details, objects, colours etc. Then when you walk around the corner and examine if everything is the same as you had expected. Is anything different? Are the walls the same colour? Does the clock have the correct time on it? Is someone in the room that you didn't expect? If something is out of place, then confirm it with a reality check, hold your nose and try to breathe through it. If you do this enough times daily, you will unquestionably find yourself doing it subconsciously in your dreams out of habit.

This same method can be done by opening doors. Before you open any door, take a moment to remember what should be behind it, then open it and check. To your surprise, you may even see a completely different room! At times, it can even be so obvious that you won't even require to perform a reality check because you'll just *know*. You can use this method outside, at work, or essentially anywhere that you're familiar with. The bottom line is; do reality checks whenever something seems strange or odd. Always be on the lookout for unusual things happening in your life. Remember yourself. Imagination and attention to detail are also essential here.

Reality checks are a great tool, but there is one issue with them if you pay enough critical attention to your awareness when you do it. In the simplest form of their practice, they are only a means of becoming lucid, perhaps a few or more times in your day. Doing a few of these a day usually only total to around one or two minutes at best when combined. After you do the reality check and conclude that you're not dreaming, most people continue their day as blind as before they remembered to do the reality check. Saying, "Okay, I'm not dreaming" which, as discussed in this book, is not entirely true. One of the first teachings in advanced dreaming practices in native American shamanism is to realise that you never stop dreaming. We are constantly creating realities unconsciously or consciously.

Alternatively, you can use the following reality check when questioning your reality, "Am I in the non-physical?", or "Am I in the astral?". The former is more effective because we can be completely unconscious at any point in our lives, unaware of whether we are in the physical, dreams or in the astral. We are unaware because we are constantly dreaming and attached to our fantasies, dramas, imagined past or future, or reactions towards others etc. It is essential to realise whether we are in physical or non-physical reality that we are dreaming in either dimension. For example, one may be in the physical, and you may even think that your mind is silent because you cannot hear any inner chatter when you direct your focus inwards. But the reality is that on some level, you are still dreaming the dream of your life, or perhaps even dreaming or thinking that you are meditating and becoming a 'spiritual person' instead of actually just *Being*; it is important to be aware of all the content of your 'physical dream life' just as it is important to be mindful of your dreams while asleep. Otherwise, we will undoubtedly not know the difference.

When you ask yourself, "Am I in the non-physical?" you do not imply to your mind that it is not a dream. We must live as though we are always in the dream of our minds, because we *are*, and to walk through the spiritual path is to walk through our path of dreams that we've set out for ourselves and come out on the other side into greater self-realised realities.

From the moment you started learning names about everyday objects and concepts, your mind began forming the dream of life. When you look at a tree, do you see the tree through the filter of ideas through your mind, or do you really *see* the tree? In practice, you may think that there is not much to this type of 'seeing'. However, if one was to truly awaken their consciousness while looking at a tree, they would realise the profound significance and learn a multitude of information about nature conveyed by the tree - just in the same way that great minds in the past were able to make observations that others were previously unconscious of. For example, Isaac Newton noticing that gravity existed through simply observing apples falling from a tree.

Furthermore, through observing a tree in this way, you would see how you are not separate from the tree and that the tree is not separate from you. One can come to realisations like this by looking at anything, but alas, we have the battles of our own minds and preoccupations before we can even get to a degree of inner silence which is tranquil enough to be sensitive to that type of information.

One can become so proficient and sensitive to this type of seeing that they don't just receive complex understanding from looking at things, but they can also receive visions and perceive the multidimensional realities of such forms, that is, to see its essence, where it came from and other types of information. You may even see its past or future, or you may even be able to communicate with it, ask it questions and receive clear answers in return. This is more understandable when we do it in the astral plane, but it is also possible in the physical plane too. Many 'extrasensory' abilities like this can be understood in the astral plane, such as clairvoyance, clairaudience and clairsentience. You can naturally pick up and practice these things the more you spend time in the astral plane and interact with other beings and lifeforms.

The greatest minds in history are the ones who have realised the power of such an 'inner intelligent sensitivity'; they realised that in order to pursue the secrets of the universe by merely using learned concepts of the mind is a sure way to find unsure and weak results. Such known geniuses all have this in common; they are conscious of their own thoughts and feelings and are as much disidentified with them as they are conscious of them. They realised this and drew their influence from that which gives our minds and feelings power; the source – consciousness.

"A human being is a part of the whole called by us universe, a part limited in time and space. He experiences himself, his thoughts and feeling as something separated from the rest, a kind of optical delusion of his consciousness. This delusion is a kind of prison for us, restricting us to our personal desires and to affection for a few persons nearest to us. Our task must be to free ourselves from this prison by widening our circle of compassion to embrace all living creatures and the whole of nature in its beauty."

- *Albert Einstein*

Exercise 2: Reality Checks

1. Take a few conscious breaths and become acutely aware of your physical body and surroundings, become present. Where are you? What are you doing?
2. Prepare yourself to do a reality check of your own choosing, but before you do it, scan your surroundings slowly and mindfully, letting your eyes look at everything in your surroundings, look for any signs of anything strange, notice if your mind is *assuming* whether you're in the physical. Consider what you were just doing moments ago and what events led you to be where you are now.
3. Really consider for a moment that you one-hundred percent, without a doubt, could be in a non-physical environment; think about what you will do next if you discover that you are. Then, with this honest consideration in your heart, perform the reality check vigorously. Do it a few times just to be sure.
4. If you find yourself in a non-physical reality, carry out your intentions. If you are in physical reality, be aware of your mind continuing to assume that you're not in a dream and try your best not to allow your reality check to be a reason to lower your awareness of your surroundings. Stay present, and intend to do another reality check in an hour or so.
5. Repeat this practice as many times as you can throughout the day. The more you do it throughout the day, the greater you increase your chances of doing it while dreaming. Make

sure you are consistent, and always do it before you sleep and when you wake up.

If you follow these steps intensely and diligently, you will find there is a feeling of 'aliveness' that can arise from this; explore it and surrender to the feeling. It is also good to practice before and after meditation. If you are persistent with this practice and do it enough times over the course of a week, it is highly likely that you will find yourself doing it in a dream or unconscious OBE.

MEMORY & RECALL IS CRUCIAL

It's great to practice lucid dreaming and astral projection, but frankly, it's absolutely useless if you can't remember your experiences. Seriously, you could already be having potentially life-changing and deeply meaningful experiences already, but you just may not be remembering them. I've had many profound experiences where I didn't remember them till after twelve hours of being awake. So, make sure it's the very first thing you prioritise every morning. Personally, I can remember anywhere up to around eight unique dreams some mornings.

One core principle is that you must pay attention to your insignificant dreams. The reason many don't bother remembering dreams is because they think they have no meaning. Yet, if you pay enough attention, you can find meaning even in the most insignificant ones. When you wake up, do not move your body; even if you open your eyes, close them. Don't let thoughts about upcoming activities of the day enter your mind just yet. Relax and meditate while laying down and aim to remember any experiences you had throughout the night.

It's said that if we move our physical bodies as soon as we wake, we disengage ourselves further from our astral energies and struggle more to recall what happened throughout the night. I can't emphasise this enough; remember your dreams – especially the inconsequential ones! Trying to recall all the details of your 'irrelevant' dreams will make your memory stronger instead of just recalling the ones that are easy to remember. Even ordinary people remember their 'interesting' dreams. Don't just write off the 'boring' ones—endeavour to recall all of them in perfect clarity. Whether you're having a lucid dream or astral projection, before going back to your physical body, play through every moment of your experience in your mind, then wake up, don't move, and go through the scenes again in your mind. Then record it either by using a voice recorder or write it in a journal - which can be on a physical paper journal or an electronic device such as a mobile phone. Listen to, or read over your experiences from the past few days every night before sleep. If you're consciously in a dream or OBE, recalling your experiences while out of the body before waking up, drastically secures your memories in your awareness, and you'll remember considerably more detail as if it was a memory from the physical when you wake up. Non-physical memory is a psychic muscle that we need to use and exercise daily, or it will become weak. So, wake up and replay the experience, then replay it in your journal, then replay again before you next go to sleep… replay, replay, replay!

Another way you can improve your memory and clarity is that when you're out of body, study something visually in detail for a moment. I usually examine the palm of my hands. You'll be surprised at the level of detail in the astral. Every time you do it, it solidifies your conviction that you're in a tangible, concrete location in a very real experience. When we give attention to detail in the astral plane, we greatly boost the clarity of the experience, especially when you realise that the level of detail in the astral is far beyond anything possible in the physical. Whether gazing at the floor beneath you, looking closely at a brick wall, or feeling the textures of a tree with your hands; this can all intensify your awareness and ground you in whatever dimension you find yourself in.

WAKING BACK TO BED

'Waking back to bed' is a common phrase amongst both lucid dreaming and astral projection communities and teachings. The phrase generally means going to bed, sleeping, waking up after around four to six hours of sleep, and then going back to sleep after a short time of being awake; it's best to meditate during this time, which is an effective way to solidify your intentions, you can use affirmations during the meditation.

What this does is it jolts your waking awareness tricking your brain into thinking it's ready for the day, when in reality, you're about to go back to sleep as your physical body is still tired. However, you'll be bringing that conscious wakefulness to your sleep. This enables you to become much more likely to be aware of your dreams or go straight into astral projection. So many variations of the 'Wake-Back-To-Bed' (WBTB) method is taught throughout numerous major OBE teachings, and for good reason. The physical body and mind require deep sleep to restore energy. If you've been unsuccessful for a while, I highly recommend employing 'WBTB' as a better schedule for your attempts. When we wake up in the middle of the night, we're less inclined to overthink due to being in a 'drowsy' state; you want to maintain this state while you wake up, meditate, and go back to sleep.

One important factor, if you are really determined, is to be consistent. Consistency doesn't just apply to WBTB but to all the exercises given in this book. Being consistent creates momentum, persistence and dedication; the subconscious is formed through all of these aspects, through habit.

If you can do WBTB every night combined with meditation, you will significantly enhance your chances of being successful. Depending on your age and who you are, your body will begin to come out of deep sleep after anywhere between four to six hours and go into its REM cycle. Practising WBTB will give you a feel of how many hours is best for you. Waking up and getting out of bed boosts REM patterns where we can more potently employ a 'mind awake, body asleep' approach. Personally, I find I require around 6 hours of sleep. I wake up, meditate anywhere from twenty minutes to an hour, and then go back to sleep, continuing my meditative, drowsy state, grounded in intent. Even if you're not successful with this method every night, I find it guarantees you to have at least vivid dreams ninety percent of the time. Vivid dreams make greater impressions on our memory and emotions and can even often hold significant meaning for us, establishing a firmer connection to the non-physical.

Exercise 3: Waking Back to Bed

1. Before you sleep, set an alarm to trigger anywhere after between four to six hours of sleep. If you are more determined and not too busy the next day, set it to trigger every two hours so that you can maximise your attempts.
2. Go to sleep as you regularly would with the intent of waking up in the middle of your sleep cycle in order to astral project. Be calm, relaxed and well-rested.
3. When your alarm wakes you up, immediately remember yourself and your intent for astral projection.
4. Get up out of bed, and walk around slowly. The point here is to gather your thoughts and intent clearly. If you have experience with meditation, you can employ the

slow Zen-like focus which is often taught in so many Eastern meditation teachings. One crucial factor you need to keep in mind is to stay sleepy and drowsy so that your physical body can easily fall back to sleep.

5. After anywhere between ten to thirty minutes of being awake (experiment with what's best for you), go back to bed.
6. Repeat to yourself as you sleep, "I WILL come out of body".
7. Upon awakening, do not move and recall any dreams or experiences you had, then record them into a journal or voice memo.

MEDITATION AS A PREREQUISITE TO ASTRAL PROJECTION

Up until now, we have explored the idea that what we currently know as reality is actually a matter of dealing with dreams and illusions in our perception. So, why does meditation matter, and where does it fall into astral projection? You could say that meditation provides the bridge for us to walk across, with the perception of dreams at the beginning and the deeper dimensions of conscious realities at the other side. When one first starts out on the path of awakening consciousness, we usually make progress and think to ourselves, "Wow! I have found enlightenment, reality!" yet when one continues, they find even more profound levels of reality which make the previously found dimensions of consciousness seem more like a dream in comparison. This is called spiritual growth. In this way, enlightenment and dimensions of consciousness are processes by which we internally travel closer and closer towards what Buddhists call The Great Reality, or Absolute Reality, or what is often referred to as The Source in esoteric teachings. Until we reach that point, most of what we see still has some form of illusion, even in the astral. Still, even the closest dimensions, which are under just a few layers beyond our current one, are highly beneficial and liberating for us to experience; the practice is always one step at a time.

Meditation is the active process of sifting through layers of mental and emotional turbulence. It is not about becoming something, but removing that which we have learned and been conditioned by - overcoming the inner obstacles that already lie in our path. For if we did not have these obstacles, then we would already be fully awakened beings, and there would be no path to walk in the first place.

Deep meditation deserves a dedicated book for itself, but in short, if you aren't meditating already, yet practising astral projection with little success, then I highly recommend making a start. Meditation does a fantastic job of anchoring us in the present moment; in *Being* and awareness. Even if it seems there's a lot of mental noise at first, being consistent and patient will bear fruits. You will see that by simply becoming aware of this mental noise, space will gradually grow in your consciousness, and you will begin to have spontaneous realisations about yourself in ways you never previously understood.

By 'consistent' I mean try to devote yourself to at least ten minutes a day of formal meditation for at least a month, and see where it takes you from there and how it affects your dreams, not to mention how it will also positively impact your life, focus and overall happiness and relationships.

Don't try to force control over your thoughts; proper control comes naturally. After many weeks of consistent meditation, you'll feel your mind is becoming a serene and still lake, centred in your heart, and you'll intuitively feel when you can peacefully decline unwanted thoughts entering your consciousness. You'll find many meditation teachers telling you that you shouldn't 'control' your thoughts. While that's true, they should actually be specifying that you shouldn't stop your thoughts *forcefully*. It is actually fine to stop thinking, but it must be done peacefully, through profound comprehension that most thoughts are impractical, and at the same time by entering the experience of your present physical reality. Just one way to enter a more present way of life is by making a habit of noticing the silence between sounds, and also observing the space between objects; thus, inner silence, and inner space, arise *naturally*.

Suppose you are meditating for some time in maintained inner stillness. In that case, you may notice your body feel light and become endowed with the sensation of new energy filling your physical body. This is a type of energetic healing of your psyche and physical body simultaneously, which takes place within your 'Etheric Body', which is responsible for your physical body's general health and vitality. Do not confuse this energetic feeling with the 'vibrations' that notoriously happen before astral projection. If you notice this in meditation, there is no need to do anything, do not let it distract you, go back to the breath and continue your practice. In meditation, whatever experience unfolds, let it unfold, do not attach yourself to anything; stay in the emptiness, the void, the impermanence and formlessness of consciousness. To attach to thought-forms is to enter back into illusory perception. It is essential to flow through every moment, letting go of every thought and new emotion and every new realisation as they come. Simply acknowledge, without attaching.

Often when one finds new states of *Being* in meditation, we become overwhelmed with this new type of bliss and rejoice in it; it is great to enjoy it, but do not spoil it with attachment. Instead, honour it and let it be there for as long as it lasts. It is like trying to lure beautiful stray cats into your home; to do this, the blossoming of your consciousness opens the doors to your house, and it manifests food and catnip plants to attract them. Nothing else is required of you. Then once a cat comes in, if you are not careful, you become fascinated and attached and lose your practice, mindfulness and focus. In that case, your doors shut, and the cat no longer feels safe and disappears, or perhaps you are really desperate to 'reach' enlightenment, and you chase the cat and hold it and try to force it to love you. Whatever presents itself to you,

you have to simply allow and remain open to experience, whether it's a 'good' experience, or a 'bad' one. This is the same principle for experiencing prolonged out of body states. Don't cling on to experiences, be accepting when it presents itself to you, and be just as accepting when it leaves.

One must realise that any newly attained transcended states of consciousness are very subtle compared to our usual rigid and dense states. We must treat it and ourselves with love, care and gentleness. None of this can be forced; it is all spontaneous, as the universe is - there is a magical spontaneity to this intelligence, just like in nature where you see birds make their nests and migrate to different climates; they know what to do, and they do not require thinking. We are no different from the birds; this is harmony and grace which instinctively exists within all of us. The only thing we can do is set the atmosphere and plant the seeds of intention. This is done through prayer, meditation, spiritual contemplation etc. Everything will fall into place; you only need faith and willpower. It is comforting to realise you do not need to excessively *think* about life to achieve your goals.

Prayer is a word that has had many connotations and preconceptions attached to it over time. Many think that it is a useless practice where one asks an imagined higher entity for help. Yet, that is only a small and superficial way to understand the power of prayer. I am exploring this in this book because I believe that in understanding prayer, we understand a part of ourselves that can significantly enhances our meditation practices; that is, to meditate and pray at the same time. Meditation alone is like become an incense stick, and prayer is actually lighting the incense stick – or meditation is like becoming a singing bowl, and prayer is actually singing the bowl.

If you are the religious type and already praying to a certain God or deity, then this is no problem and asking for help with astral projection in this way can be effective; you are probably already somewhat aware of the benefits of this through your own experience. But for those new to the concept, let's take a deeper look at the mechanics of prayer.

True prayer comes from the heart; it is to energetically conjure emanations of humility, growth, insight and manifestation. Prayer is a communication of sorts with higher, but not egoically superior, intelligence of our consciousness - that which we know exists deep within us but we find hard to reach in our current level of being. Furthermore, you do not need to use words when praying. For example, if you would like to request from your consciousness to come out of your body, we do this in a serious and honouring way, full of devotion and love for the divine and mysterious beauty of existence. In this way, you attract the non-physical celestial forces of the cosmos within your *Being*. There doesn't need to be words, just think of your question and desire, and hold it in your heart. The question will burn in this powerful organ and rise like incense, solidifying your intent and expansion. So, in a way, this is a more profound and superior form of affirmations, instead of just regurgitating words like a robot. At least five minutes of physical relaxation is recommended before beginning. When you finish praying and meditating, don't habitually fall back into the state you were previously in; try to maintain your upright emotions and awareness till the next time you practice and also as you sleep. Meditation doesn't just have to be sitting down; you can meditate while doing many things.

"There is walking zen, standing zen, sitting zen, and lying zen. When you sit, just sit. When you walk, just walk."

\- *Alan Watts*

Exercise 4: Meditation for Developing an Astral Projection Mindset

1. Sit up comfortably with your spine straight but relaxed, you can use some back support as long as it doesn't make you feel too sleepy.
2. Scan your body slowly, starting from your toes to the top of your head, letting go of each part of your body, surrendering to deep relaxation. Visualise a golden light coming in through your feet and gradually consuming your entire body in deep relaxation.
3. Breathe slowly and deeply through your nostrils, into your belly, hold the breath for a few seconds and let go. Repeat at least three times. Afterwards, begin to let the breath flow naturally, without control or attachment. Just notice its natural rhythm, like a seashore coming in and out.
4. Employ your willpower to focus only on your breath and nothing else. Notice your attention waver because you either have distracting thoughts coming in, or your willpower is weak. Whenever you lose focus, just gently go back to focusing on watching the breath in a detached manner. Don't stress over the thoughts; whenever you notice a thought, just acknowledge it and keep coming back to the practice. This repetition of coming back is part of the practice, don't get upset about having a 'noisy' mind. Acceptance and patient will see you through. To strengthen your practice, you can affirm to yourself, as a sort of mantra; "I am not my mind" and "I am not my body".
5. The longer you can focus on the breath, watching it flow in and out, without becoming overwhelmed by thoughts, then the longer you are exercising controlled and sustained intent; your presence is growing.

Eventually, after months of steady practice, this presence will overflow into your non-physical realities during sleep. You can also apply this same intent to staying grounded in the astral for longer periods of time.

6. This type of meditation can go infinitely deep depending on your persistence, consistence and level of peace and silence that arises from it. Relish and thrive in it.

TRANSCENDING THE BODY

Society teaches us how to look after the physical body throughout our lives. We study science and medicine, and our parents and doctors tell us what medications to take for specific ailments. We get bruises, scratches and break our bones. One can attain all the material wealth in the world, but it can bear no value when an illness arrives. When you are ill, there is only one focus, to feel better. In modern-day, what we see emphasised in the news is what illness you *could* develop, and rarely how you can prevent them naturally.

Emotions are simply a reflection of how our body feels about thoughts in the mind. Emotions are a deeper level of thinking and intuiting. It is a disgrace that in our society, we are taught all too much to think and rarely to feel, or what's worse, we are commonly taught to feel fear through fear-based thinking, especially if one watches the news on TV often. The same goes for when many hear about astral projection. What a shame; astral projection is a remarkable ability of immeasurable possibility, yet when people hear about it, the first thing that comes to mind is fear-based thoughts when there is absolutely no need. We don't have to just change *what* we think, but *how* we think.

Awakening consciousness is synonymous with learning how to transcend the physical body through astral projection. Furthermore, transcending the physical body is absolutely synonymous with self-healing. But what is transcending the body? It is a profound realisation that you are not your body; it is when you stop identifying with the body. However, we don't transcend the body by trying to forget it; instead, we enter the body and become acutely aware of it. The body is a gateway, a temple to a higher intelligence. The same is done with the mind also. We don't transcend the mind by ignoring it, but by occupying and understanding it.

Such a thing can barely be talked about and only experienced. As repeated throughout this book, this is something that must be *experienced* beyond the mind, in your awareness. This is *gnosis*. As taught by Gnostic groups, *gnosis* is defined in its purest form as knowledge based on experienced, as opposed to belief or intellectual theory.

Prolonged and consistent meditation enables one to observe and become one with the body with no thoughts, just pure awareness. This act of rooted observation helps you innately realise that you are not your body, and in this realisation, you will be less attached, naturally. Thus, you will more easily separate from your physical body when the time comes and more easily identify with your spiritual body - the energy that animates and occupies your physical body. This is difficult to imagine only when we have a lack of practice and experience.

Can a Spirit Possess You While You're Out of Body?

You'll find a lot of misinformation and fear-mongering about this; it is all utter nonsense. Astral projection is absolutely safe and natural. There aren't many ways to actually prove that it's safe, but here are two logical points:

1. The astral body is connected to the physical body in a similar way that a radio is connected to frequencies. You can't have one without the other. PROJECTING implies one location to

another, so two locations, not just one. You can be on the other side of the galaxy but still be connected to your physical body. You could look into the 'silver cord' about this.

2. The fact that we all astral project every night unconsciously anyway implies that it is most likely safe since you don't see anyone becoming possessed, do you? In a sense, it's actually safer to practice astral projection than it is not to, because at least then you'd be conscious of what you're doing and being influenced by at night. Of course, you can't really know whether we astral project unconsciously every night until you become experienced yourself. Still, I and many authors and experienced astral projectors will agree on this.

Protection

It's first essential to understand that the best protection is one of being on a level of consciousness that naturally emanates universal and unconditional love for all beings, where fear is far from your natural state. However, here's a general guide on what you can do if you are the type of person who is still 'afraid' of things in the astral plane.

Keep an altar as a symbol to protect your home while you astral project; it should be square-shaped, with a white cloth on it. Burn a white candle on it all the time or whenever you're present in the house. Place deities or symbols you consider holy, sacred or powerful. Burn incense, preferably real frankincense or copal resin burned on charcoal discs in a clay pot. Visualise and cast a circle of fire or light of protection around your house three times. You can combine this with prayer and mantras. You can ask angels, masters, guides or any other type of positive 'astral helper' for help with protection. This will also help with experiencing fewer nightmares. I won't go into it much here, but there are thousands of beings in the astral who are committed to helping humanity with their spiritual progress. Many will listen to your call if you are genuine and sincere.

As you cast the circle of protection while visualising the fire or light, you can say something like:

> "Angels, masters and guides of the astral plane, protect this house in a spiritual camouflage so that no evil or darkness can penetrate it. Cast away all kinds of darkness and any other kinds of related evil or negative forces or energies."

You can finish this with the mantra OM or AMEN three times. Do all this with positive emotions and complete faith.

ENTERING THE ASTRAL PLANE FROM A LUCID DREAM

To turn your dreams into astral projection, you need to 'stop', 'break' or 'go beyond' the 'narrative' of the dream. To do this, whenever you find yourself lucid in a dream, look around and feel how your mind is creating the scenes; this takes practice and meditation to understand deeply. Once you recognise you're creating these scenes in your mind, it becomes easier to stop them; essentially, we're doing the same as when we wake up and stop thinking in meditation or when we 'snap back to reality' in waking life. It's all about being present. This can be done within an instant, and at the same time, remember and employ your intent to enter the astral.

So, what happens when your consciousness is in the non-physical yet isn't dreaming anymore? Well, it has no choice but to enter reality, in other words, the astral. Two things can happen when you do this; one is that you will witness the content and objects of the dream dissolve before your eyes, and you'll feel a shift in the atmosphere, which can include, but is not limited by, vibrations and hypnagogic imagery or sounds; shortly during this transitionary stage you'll most likely go straight into the astral; everything about your experience will feel different and more palpable. You'll know you're not dreaming anymore and that you've successfully entered an objective dimension. On the other hand, instead, you may go back to your body and exit the body from there. One thing to note is that if you do go back to your body with the intention of astral projecting, make sure you don't move your physical body. Any time we attempt to sit or lay down for formal meditation or astral projection, we shouldn't be moving any part of our bodies. Let it settle and become still but without frustration or restlessness, just relax.

There are different techniques for entering the astral from lucid dreams that others teach, like 'creating a portal'; these are fine, but what I'm describing is more about understanding the 'consciousness mechanics' behind what happens when we do this. Understanding is essential when turning dreams into astral projection.

Usually, I don't like to provide methods for entering the astral plane from dreams because I place a higher value on understanding this process; which derives from the direct inner knowledge that you need to innately recognise that you're creating the dream-illusions yourself and then instinctively 'stop' or 'break' the content of the dream, so that you can enter objective consciousness (meditation helps with this). With that said, however, I have discovered a particular method that I've been doing again and again while in lucid dreams to enter the astral plane; see below.

Exercise: 5: 'The Flying Method' of Turning Lucid Dreams into Astral Projection

1. Achieve lucidity in your dream by any means of the numerous lucid dreaming methods you can find out there, one of the most effective being reality check exercises.
2. Once lucid, become present and recognise the content of the dream, and without hesitation, employ your intent for astral projection, feel your 'dream' body intensely and fly upwards. You may feel vibrations and strange sounds. As you feel yourself travelling and breaking through your non-

physicality (it can be quite an intense feeling), just intend to keep ascending through higher states of awareness. You can even say mentally, "Enter the astral plane!".

3. After a period of transitioning, you will find yourself in a new environment; the difference in clarity and sensation should be astounding.

You will know whether you are in the astral and whether you're still dreaming or not. It's most likely the case that you're not dreaming if you experienced it similar to the way I described, but if you're struggling and still find yourself in a dream state, just try it again. The fact that you even recognise that you're in a dream state is excellent progress anyway. If you find yourself going back to your body, don't worry; just don't move your physical body and employ the intention to leave your body; you can do this simply by getting up (just not physically). If you're still struggling, try intending and forcing a swaying sensation in your awareness. This will help you loosen up out of your physical shell, like a chick trying to roll its egg around in an attempt to crack it.

Without thinking about it, you can just simply 'get up' or 'float up'. Do this instinctively. Just get up without moving your physical body. Don't think about it - it is straightforward in practice if you don't overanalyse it.

Training Imagination

Imagination is another significant aspect if you want to strengthen your astral projection abilities as well as your memory of it. Unfortunately, many people's imaginations are weak due to not using it enough or abusing it through excessive use of technology.

Once you're in a deep state of meditation, you can use this visualisation exercise to help strengthen your abilities. Visualising the process of coming out of body eases your mind into a taste of what will happen during an OBE, so that you won't be too staggered when it happens for real.

Exercise 6: Visualisation Practice

1. Relax your physical body. If you're having trouble relaxing or you're feeling restless, you can count to five as you inhale inwards, then hold the breath for another five seconds, and do the same with the out breath. Repeat this seven times and you should begin to feel much more comfortable.
2. Meditate for some time until you feel you are calm.
3. Without straining yourself, begin to become aware of every cell in your body; don't just think about it; feel it. Feel the energy of every part. You may have to be patient if you don't feel anything at first. Scan your body from your toes, feet, legs, groin, stomach, organs, arms, hands, neck, face, eyes, brain etc., to the top of your head.
4. Now become conscious of your entire body in one whole peripheral awareness, feel the entire energy field of your body, as if you are a sphere of energy. Say to yourself, "I am not my body".
5. Now that you have your entire body in your awareness, feel it become weightless as if there is no gravity. Then simultaneously feel and visualise yourself floating up and out of your body.
6. See the room you're in (with your mind's eye) and notice it in full detail; notice objects, colours, features etc. Take your time; controlling imagination precisely takes a bit of practice if you're not used to it, be patient and calm. Once you've analysed the first part of your room, slowly turn and look at different parts. You can do this for as long as you like, flying around your house, being aware and feeling this 'double' body that you're now using

with your mind. After some time, begin to slowly fly back to your body, seeing yourself sitting in meditation and merge back with it gradually.

7. Continue meditation and set your intentions to astral project when you next go to sleep. Trust that your subconscious will do this for you.

Remember that this exercise is NOT astral projection. It is just training your imagination and concentration in unison to get a feel for how to travel around once actually out of body.

Alternatively, you can do this same exercise by walking around your house, instead of flying. I find flying helps me maintain that 'full-body awareness'; the same sensation happens when I actually fly in the astral. After three days of doing this exercise daily, I basically guarantee you will see vast improvements in your dreams' vividness, your ability to recall scenes in detail, and your ability to stay present for longer once you're consciously out of your body; all this inevitably gives dreams and astral projections greater impressions on your mind, vastly improving your memory of them.

TRANSCENDING THE MIND

Generally speaking, transcending the body is more straightforward than transcending the mind. This is because, through the mind, we can observe that it can say "I have a body". Accordingly, the 'I' that says it owns a body is implying separateness through its sense of ownership. So, through detaching from the body, you may feel like you 'own a body', but who are *you*? *You* do not own anything; your body simply is - and so too with your mind. The significance to realise here is that awareness and mind are not one and the same. The fact that we can also *observe* our mind implies that the *observer* of it is closer to the truer reality of ourselves. In meditation, there is the observer and the observed. We can *see* that we have a body. The same effect is true for our minds, but since the mind is something we cannot see physically, it is harder for us to grasp because of our non-physical attachment to the mind and its identifications.

Imagine for a moment that a man creates a small advanced device that echoes everything he says, and not just that, but it records everything in his life like a video camera does, and he can play back scenes whenever he likes by simply willing it. On top of this, the device is so powerful, it can play back hundreds of images, sounds and videos, with infinite storage capacity. The man then attaches this device inside his head. As he goes about his day with this incredible and revolutionary tool, he enjoys being able replay scenes to study them in-depth and is able to do many things at once.

Others marvel at his newly found cleverness and praise him. The man loves his device so much, which has enabled him to analyse and create more things than anyone else. He loves his 'mind-tool' more than anything in the world. However, after many years of use, he becomes so absorbed in this tool that he forgets that he even created it, and not only that, but the tool becomes so dysfunctional and out of control that he cannot turn it off anymore.

The device starts constantly playing multiple videos and images all at the same time. The man becomes overwhelmed and upset and cannot choose what videos to pay attention to anymore. Thus, he is no longer the controller of this tool and falls to the mercy of it – he falls BELOW the level of the mind. He becomes depressed and solemn and falls victim to any sense-perception presented by this 'mind-tool' that is running rampant. This leads to all sorts of physical and mental illnesses. Emotions are the reactions to our thoughts, and when we do not like or do not want specific thoughts because we lack control, we often develop negative emotions. In turn, developing negative feelings in our body which give rise to 'dis-ease' (disease). The emotion of 'ease' is great medicine, not 'dis-ease'.

If the man is not careful and becomes too consumed by this tool, he may begin to not be able to identify the illusions of his mind-tool from reality; this is when we call a person insane. The mind is a tool of reflection, the ability to recognise oneself and the world through a mirror, but the mind is so powerful that we unconsciously create many mirrors, and mirrors within mirrors, and mirrors battling against mirrors within us for power. The mirrors take a mind of their own and crave our attention; this is essentially the root of addiction and compulsion. This is what Buddhists call Maya; illusion, or delusion.

This is the state of a large portion of humanity's mind today in varying degrees. If higher dimensional beings were to visit Earth and hear the general noise in the mental dimension of Earth, they would hear so much suffering and excessive and unharmonious noise. The mind creates our reality, and this type of chaotic noise is reflected and manifested in our physical world in the form of endless television channels and the internet.

The mind is a wonderful tool, a beautiful gift from creation that allows us to comprehend the mysteries of the universe through its facility of thought and reflection. But we must tame its power.

Meditation not only means you do not contribute to this old dysfunctional way of thinking, but you also generate a space and help a new way of thinking for others. This may be hard to believe since it is something you cannot perceive physically, but psychically, you generate a momentum of peace and stillness, no matter how small or subconscious its effects are.

Today, as humanity becomes even more dysfunctional, uncertain and spiritually lost, we are seeing many individuals and groups becoming more and more 'insane'. However, amidst this craziness, more and more individuals are spontaneously breaking the barriers of the limited mind through intense suffering and seeking spiritual liberation as a result of this. This happens when a soul cannot tolerate any more suffering, and they suddenly surrender all their self-loathing and self-importance. However, don't let your mind trick you into thinking that intense suffering is an excuse or effective method to awakening consciousness. You will only experience pain through this. In fact, you will learn far more soberly and intelligently by doing the work daily and meditating with conscious effort, and not only that, but you will help others along the way.

"We either make ourselves miserable, or we make ourselves strong. The amount of work is the same."

- *Don Juan Matus (Carlos Castaneda)*

PROFOUND MEDITATION

The breath, silence and darkness; the reality to which these words point to are comprehended in deep meditation. The Hebrew word 'nefeš', literally meaning 'breath,' is the word most often translated as 'soul' in the Bible. Hence, the breath becomes a powerful portal into the non-physical when awareness is placed upon it and gently concentrated for extended periods of time.

Meditation is an undoing of layers of the mind by doing absolutely nothing at all. You only need to be persistent and patient. There is nothing you need to *do* in meditation. The mind will settle; this is irrefutable, wholly and utterly true - you will experience it if you genuinely put your heart in it instead of just 'experimenting'. All you need to do is be, let be, and let go. Do not go into unconscious dreams; do not *look* for experiences or 'new states'. Simply allow consciousness to unfold and flow naturally; it knows what to do.

There is nothing more powerful, more transcending than true, profound and deep meditation. And when you understand it, it is so simple; there is nothing you need to do, yet everything gets done. All you do is sit there and observe, through such an act, one naturally penetrates through layers of muck and nonsense of the mind and finds themself in more blissful and clearer states. Meditation, in a sense, *is* conscious astral projection, that is; returning to *reality* and awakening from the dreams of the mind here and now. Enlightenment is not about becoming more or better, but becoming less of all the created conditioning in our mind.

Patience and acceptance in meditation are also vital. If your mind is doubting or is sceptical, so what? Let it be like that; it does not mean that you, consciousness, awareness, needs to be doubtful or sceptical too. Remember, you are not your mind; this is a liberating and profound thing to realise, and it's something most people would not even begin to understand.

Sometimes, even my mind becomes sceptical or doubtful, but I just observe it, smile, and carry on my day or meditation. I know that those thoughts are essentially not *me*. The mind always presents us with perceptions, but it's up to us as to what we identify with. The mind is like a child craving attention all the time, and if we give it attention to certain behaviours (i.e. doubt or fear), then it only proceeds to do more of that. However, if we stop feeding it with our attention, it eventually gives up, and that ego which previously wanted our attention so badly essentially dies – but be vigilant, new egos can always be formed again at any moment if you forget yourself and allow your integrity to waver.

When you meditate, simply observe your thoughts and feelings and go back to the breath. If any thought comes in, simply go back to the breath… do you get even more disturbing thoughts? Just go back to the breath! This 'tug of war' doesn't seem effective at first, but if you're firm and persevere, you'll transcend deeper levels of your mind through realising you have the power to not feed certain thoughts or vices with your attention anymore; thus, you gain self-control and personal power.

Every time you make an effort to come back to the present moment of the breath, you are gradually training your mind to become more tranquil and controlled; in this state, the mind becomes a far more effective tool. Through not giving useless thoughts our energy anymore, we begin to save energy for ourselves. With more spiritual energy, there's an intelligence that arises which you can recognise from the level of peace and inner silence that you gradually generate. This takes time and conscious, consistent effort - just like earning money in the physical, we only see results when we put in the work.

"What you accept, you go beyond"

– *Eckhart Tolle*

THE OBSTACLE OF THE EGO

It's fantastic if we can work on spiritual practices such as meditation and astral projection. Nevertheless, a common obstacle we all share can significantly inhibit our progress, and it's the infamous ego. This topic deserves a dedicated book for itself in order to really analyse and comprehend in its truest psychological depths. Nonetheless, let's briefly touch upon how the ego stands in the way of our progress in terms of astral projection; it can impact our progress because if we're angry, lustful, hateful, irritable, impatient, restless, impulsive, glutinous etc. throughout the day, such things can break your stream of continued spiritual efforts and disturb your mind from its accumulated peace and intentions. This happens because such psychological traits are often a result of unconscious, uncontrolled impulses.

This might sound like a challenging aspect, but there is a positive side to this. Once we recognise our negative tendencies and faults, we can actually use these bad habits and reactions that we have throughout the day for opportunities to grow in consciousness. For example, say a man comes back from work and becomes irritated when his wife doesn't have food ready for him. For his sake, it can be damaging if he becomes irritated internally, but what's destructive is if he doesn't make an effort to become conscious in that moment; his irritation can turn into anger, then out of impulsiveness, he can express his anger verbally, and if this man hasn't even a single rational thought, he could express his rage physically. The consequence of this is that now this man's previously pleasant state of mind has been agitated. The remnants of his anger may stay imprinted in his mind until he sleeps and can truly let go of the stress of the day through sleep, which is just one purpose of sleep. Suppose this man is interested in dream-related practices. In that case, he will either find it hard to become lucid, or he will only remember dreams related to his earlier emotional turmoil.

If we come into a situation that really 'hurt' us during the day, and we spent the day in self-pity after an argument, or because we became distressed by something we read or saw on the news, then we will most likely dream about it at night. Dreams act as a way for our consciousness to process impressions from the day in order to be ready for the next day. Therefore, if we don't let impressions from the day be interpreted as stressful or negative in our minds, then we have better chances of coming out of body or becoming lucid in our dreams. Similarly, people who say they had a 'bad' sleep, or have recurring nightmares, may have lived through an experience at any time in the past that gave them an impression so strong that their consciousness is struggling to 'digest' or accept it. Thus, it becomes part of their underlying subconscious reality which can express itself in various ways through behaviour. This is why consistent meditation and working on oneself can become a healing process long-term.

It's not enough to just stop acting outwardly from anger or other negative emotions; in such moments, we should look within and become highly aware of these emotions; catching them before they grow and overwhelm us. When you feel disturbing emotions or reactions try to overcome you, you can ask yourself, "Is becoming angry/irritated/depressed worth destroying my inner peace?", you can affirm to yourself, "Nothing can overwhelm me". Always try to see the bigger picture; most of what people do or say ultimately doesn't matter in the greater reality of life; it will all pass; hold onto your inner peace.

There are numerous opportunities to challenge ourselves throughout the day; it could be to do with laziness, eating too many sweet treats, watching too much TV, interacting with demanding family members etc. Exercise control over your reactions and impulses. Every challenge is an opportunity to become more aware and overcome negative tendencies that cause depression, anger or moods. We all have our triggers, and when we encounter them, we either become less conscious or more conscious, depending on the skill and strength of our control over these tendencies that arise in our awareness.

Furthermore, it's important not to see these opportunities, or 'triggers', as inherently 'bad' in daily life. If we didn't have them, we wouldn't be able to discover ourselves effectively; the world is a mirror reflecting back all parts of ourselves, the good, but also the bad. In Gnosticism, this is called the 'psychological gym of life', and it is considered a powerful tool to dissolve our egos – as opposed to just running off to a temple in the East to seclude yourself off from society, which would barely give any challenges or show yourself unconscious reactions that are within, especially when you don't have to deal with other people anymore.

"The best method for the elimination of the ego is found in everyday life lived intensively."

- *Samael Aun Weor*

Unquestionably, it's difficult for many of us to self-reflect and even more difficult to admit we have faults. This is the human dilemma, and you have to understand it's a natural part of our experience because; if we didn't have darkness within, there wouldn't even be a spiritual path to walk in the first place. There wouldn't be a journey where we have to make efforts to shine the light of awareness into dark and unknown territories of our consciousness because otherwise, everything would be light already, and you wouldn't have any desire to even read this book. What would be the point in the spiritual journey of the human being if we didn't have darkness within us to begin with?

To really take a look at our egoic patterns takes sincerity, honesty and humility, combined with living life alert and aware at all times. Such a practice, where we deny ourselves, may seem like a weak act to us initially, but it is a sure step in the path of gaining true spiritual strength; by doing so, you will also notice how it will positively and profoundly impact your nightly experiences, instilling them with more meaning as you progress, rather than having random and meaningless OBEs.

"The ego cannot dissolve itself, but in the light of awareness, it dissolves."

- *Eckhart Tolle*

The Power of Being Present

From what I've seen, meditation and being present in daily life is commonly overlooked in astral projection communities. In reality, it's my understanding that in former times, yogis and monks would naturally discover the deeper realities of the astral plane without any prior knowledge of it. They practised in the order of; meditation, lucid dreaming and then astral projection. They did this by staying present from moment to moment, treating life as one long meditation, and endeavoured to comprehend any personal psychological defects and illusions that got in their way.

For most people, except for a few gifted individuals, it's not particularly productive to jump straight into astral projection. Learn the steps, study and practice; there is no rush. Actually, there are many accounts of people who were only concerned with meditation and enlightenment, and because they were so devoted to it, they, to their surprise, naturally began having spontaneous out of body experiences without even knowing what OBEs were in the first place!

If you're someone who frequently 'fails' at astral projection, and becomes confused or upset afterwards, don't be discouraged! The fact that you're at least trying says many positive things about you. As mentioned, approaching astral projection in a gradual and wholesome way will ultimately transform you into someone who has regular spontaneous out of body experiences throughout the rest of their lives, instead of just one or two insignificant experiences here and there. The work you put in is absolutely worth it.

"Realise deeply that the present moment is all you have. Make the *Now* the primary focus of your life. Life is now. There was never a time when your life was not now, nor will there ever be."

- *Eckhart Tolle*

CULTIVATING YOUR APPROACH

Only a miniscule part of the reality of astral projection is understood logically. In fact, it is best comprehended from the right side of our brain, the side that cannot explain things logically; it's the part that appreciates the art and beauty of life. People who consciously astral project are, in essence, artists. Thus, it is my understanding we should approach it in this way, much like how a talented painter approaches their canvas. Ask any talented composer how they created such beautiful symphonies. Did they study the theories and science of music? Yes, but did Mozart or Beethoven systematically think about these things when they performed such beautiful, otherworldly compositions at the height of their careers? I would argue they certainly did not. The theories and science were deep in their subconscious by then, and when it came time to actually create music, they used their hearts, and it's with this intelligent organ that we should approach the phenomena of astral projection.

More than ever, there is so much information on the internet about the stages and sensations that occur during astral projection. Many people overanalyse these sensations too much, thinking that they need to 'think' about all these processes in a logical way. It's like asking yourself, "How do I walk?" and saying, "Well, I should get up, place my feet on the ground and try to bend one knee, and then lift one foot", but then you fall over through excessive *thinking* instead of *doing*. Walking requires the balance and awareness of your entire body; if you're going to focus on one part without balancing other parts, then you're going to fall. Likewise, we need to recognise that astral projection is a wholesome, holistic, organic, natural and integral part of our lives, just like walking. Just as babies learn to walk without thinking, we too should primarily approach astral projection in the same instinctive way.

Believe You Can Astral Project

Like many in the modern world, most people will only believe something when they see it. Hence the age-old saying, "Believing is seeing." I like this mindset; it's objective, and I don't want to draw conclusions about reality until I experience and know it for myself directly – this is *gnosis*, knowledge based on direct experience rather than belief. Nevertheless, I must admit that for me to have started having out of body experiences, I had to take a leap of faith and apply the power of belief. It is incredibly beneficial to believe in order to project. If you're having issues with scepticism and fail in intuiting the reality behind astral projection, then attempt to allow the mind to have the courage to let go of suspicion for some time. In this way, we can forget the saying, 'Seeing is Believing', and employ 'Believing is Seeing'.

Overanalysing, as the mind is so commonly taught to do, can lead to doubt. If you want to experience astral projection, my personal advice is to reduce asking yourself too many questions. Nobody can really explain the experience of astral projection fully and do it justice in words. Whether you believe or don't believe in astral projection, both are mere beliefs; the depth of reality behind it is something the intellectual mind simply cannot comprehend until it starts to witness it for itself. Have confidence and know that you *will* learn to experience it for yourself. Reality is never what our minds imagine it to be, no matter what the situation in life.

So, one's first step is often in believing, based on faith and intuition. After you experience it, you no longer need belief because it turns into direct knowledge. You have to take a leap of faith, like a blindfolded initiate in the temples of Freemasonry, Theosophy, Gnosticism, Rosicrucians etc. Those ceremonies are simply a reflection of this inner process of acquiring spiritual knowledge within all of us.

Don't Identify with Thoughts

It's essential to root ourselves in consciousness rather than the surface layer of our lives; thoughts. Yet, what are these thoughts? They're objects, or forms, floating around in the space of our consciousness. For enlightenment, it's essential for us to be rooted in formlessness, to have more space in our consciousness rather than objects; this requires a sort of 'spatial' or 'peripheral' awareness in our daily lives, rather than focusing or getting lost in certain thought-forms which present themselves to us compulsively; the mind is inherently dysfunctional in this way, and we inevitably become more dysfunctional the more we identify with every thought that enters our psychological space. Let's look at the old philosophical saying, "I think; therefore I am." by Descartes. There's an error here which you can try to identify, clarified beautifully below.

"The philosopher Descartes believed he had found the most fundamental truth when he made his famous statement: "I think, therefore I am." He had, in fact, given expression to the most basic error: to equate thinking with *Being*, and identity with thinking. It took almost 300 years before another famous philosopher saw something in that statement that Descartes, as well as everybody else, had overlooked. His name was Jean-Paul Sartre. He looked at Descartes' statement "I think, therefore I am" very deeply and suddenly realised, in his own words, "The consciousness that says 'I am' is not the consciousness that thinks." What did he mean by that? When you are aware that you are thinking, that awareness is not part of thinking. It is a different dimension of consciousness. And it is that awareness that says, "I am." If there were nothing but thought in you, you wouldn't even know you are thinking. You would be like a dreamer who doesn't know he is dreaming. You would be as identified with every thought as the dreamer is with every image in the dream."

- *Eckhart Tolle*

Cultivate Unbending Intent

Now that we've covered the importance of space-orientated consciousness, we should have a better instinct on how we can manage and master our thoughts, will and desires more gracefully. One of the most critical aspects of astral projection, which also applies to any spiritual practice, is intent. 'Intent' is how we prime our subconscious and trust our 'doing' self to act for us, while we, consciousness, remain calm in 'non-doing'.

In Carlos Castaneda books, the Native American shaman, Don Juan Matus, concludes many of his teachings by describing successful spiritual people from his time as 'Impeccable warriors with unbending intent.'

"Impeccability begins with a single act that has to be deliberate, precise and sustained. If that act is repeated long enough, one acquires a sense of unbending intent which can be applied to anything else. If that is accomplished, the road is clear. One thing will lead to another until the warrior realises his full potential. Anything is possible if one wants it with unbending intent and you don't let your thoughts interfere."

Don Juan Matus goes on to say:

> "The problem for you as a challenge is whether or not you will be capable of developing your *will*, or the power of your second attention to focus indefinitely on anything you want."

This 'second attention' from a native American perspective is the same as your subconscious *will*, your ally, which you can rely on if nurtured well. So how do we cultivate our intent? Continue your love, curiosity, passion and interest for astral projection; devote yourself, pray, meditate and penetrate it to every core of your being and leave no room for doubt. "Free your mind", as Morpheus from The Matrix said. He also says, "There's a difference between knowing the path and walking the path." So, walk the path and practice, practice, practice! Every night, as you fall to sleep, you can repeat to yourself, "I WILL astral project!", keep saying this and feel it in every cell of your being until sleep overcomes you, and without knowing how, you may find yourself coming out of body.

Willpower is an essential key to astral projection, and actually, you can achieve astral projection by willpower and intent alone, without any other particular method, if you exercise it unceasingly enough. If you are very determined, you can practice desiring to astral project all day, on all levels of your mind. If you really want to do it, it will happen. Thinking about astral projection in this way, knowing that you will astral project, buries the intent deep into your unconscious and conscious mind that you will inevitably astral project spontaneously one day. You have to want it, crave it, long for it in your soul, even when you're at work, at school, shopping, cleaning your house or having a conversation with your boss. Contemplate the astral in your daily life; reflect on the connection between the physical and astral worlds, and be aware of its significance in existence. It is always around us, just as there is oxygen in the air. It is within us and an integral part of our nature. For example, the astral dimension holds within it the non-physical forces and feelings that we share with other people.

Additionally, as another tip for intent, it's essential to be specific about why and what you want to achieve from visiting the astral plane. This means having a particular task that you want to undertake when you next find yourself out of body. Having an intent such as "I want to do whatever is best" is fine, but if your intent is vague, then your experience will also be vague. Have a specific wish you really crave to explore! It could be to investigate your past lives, contact a deceased relative, find out about Earth's future, talk to a guide, or visit another planet. The possibilities are endless, but the important part is it should be something you emotionally desire; only then will the power of your heart help you. After all, the astral plane is commonly called the 'Emotional Plane' in various esoteric texts. Doing this will anchor your consciousness in willpowered purpose. It will significantly increase your chances of having a detailed, significant and prolonged journey, instead of walking around aimlessly, which generally results in shorter and less meaningful experiences.

TRYING TOO HARD

Analysing Attempts

One of the most common phrases and problems I see expressed amongst novices in astral projection goes along the lines of:

"… so I got to the vibrational stage, and then I tried to get out of body, but I couldn't do it."

To me, this kind of thought process has potential issues you may want to reflect on. If you've ever thought of something similar, consider how this way of thinking can affect your experience. I'm not saying there's anything wrong with thinking such a thought, but I am saying critically analysing it can help you understand your progress. Let's break it down:

"I got to the vibrational stage…"

It's okay to acknowledge what sensations happened; however, try not to think in terms of 'stages'; there are no concrete steps or stages to do with astral projection. Don't expect the same sensation to happen again or whether it will happen in any same particular order; astral projection doesn't need to have all the typical sensations you hear about every time you astral project! It can be different each time or have minimal sensations, especially if you go straight into the astral plane from a lucid dream.

"... and then I tried to get out of body"

If you're feeling vibrations and feel like you're about to come out of body, but you keep ruining the experience by 'trying' something prematurely, then stop trying. As Yoda from Star Wars said, "Do or do not, there is no try." When you're about to come out of body, you can usually feel vibrations, hear sounds, or see visuals; don't worry about them. Don't try to 'grab' onto new sensations immediately like a child in a candy store; instead, be patient, surrender to them and let them unfold naturally; in this way, you can eventually intensify them. Once intensified, you should be able to lean into those sensations and just 'get up' out of your body. If you can't, don't worry, it doesn't mean you've failed; just go back to noticing the sensations and immerse yourself in them, and then try again a few moments later. Just maintain your awareness, willpower and intent; that's all you need to do. In meditation, when a new thought comes in, would you follow it immediately and aimlessly? No – the principle of meditation practice is to maintain your awareness in a calm and detached manner; this is the same for hypnagogic sensations during astral projection. When it's time, don't 'try', just 'do', and get up out of your body! Do not think about it.

"... but I couldn't do it."

Firstly, don't be disheartened; Rome wasn't built in a day. Consistency is critical; maintain your efforts, and you will reap the rewards. People think they are 'failing at attempts'. However, every attempt or any effort will contribute to your progress no matter how long you've been trying. It's all part of the learning experience, and the fact you are making efforts is enough reason to give yourself credit.

Secondly, due to mostly cultural conditioning, our minds have been hardwired to think we must 'do' something in order to achieve a result. Again, don't interpret this completely literally. Of course, you are *doing* something - attempting to astral project. However, paradoxically, it is wise to prioritise non-doing as a means to that end. So, how do we achieve anything if we're always in a state of 'non-doing' during the attempt? This is where we prime our subconscious to do it for us, which we cultivate through faith, willpower and intent.

Exiting The Body

Now that I've attempted to convince you to stop trying so hard to leave the body let's actually address how to approach leaving the body when the time comes! At some point during your endeavours, you will successfully find yourself feeling extrasensory vibrations, sounds, and/or images. This usually happens between the precise moment of wakefulness and sleep. There is a point where you do actually need to attempt to exit the body, but it's a subtle art to know when it's okay to do so. Usually, the correct time is when all these extrasensory phenomena become very intense and seem to reach their peak. This takes practice, and you'll get a feel for it in time. My direct advice is whenever you do attempt to 'float up', 'get up', or 'roll out' of your physical body, notice whether the sensations become weaker, and if they do, stop and just carry on being aware of the sensations, and then after a few moments, they should strengthen again and you can re-attempt your exit. Make sure you calmly focus on the sensations and allow them to intensify; they should get more substantial and louder! Only then is the right time to split yourself from your physical body.

It's like boiling milk in a pan on a hob to pour it into a mug. The milk is your consciousness, the hob is the power of your meditative intent, the pan is your physical body, and the mug is your astral body. Cook the milk patiently; take it off the hob too early, and it's not ready; you won't have enough power in your milk. Take it off too late, and it boils over the pan with too much energy, and you lose milk. But if you take it off just at the right time, you have a nice warm drink to be poured into the mug; it's not too hot that your awareness becomes erratic and uncontrollable, and it's not too cold that you struggle to maintain a calm focus.

The vibrational state is absolutely not a physical sensation. Although it can feel like you're experiencing an earthquake, it's just your astral body 'activating'. To be honest, I think the word 'vibrations' has been very misleading for some people. Remember - in order to astral project, your physical body needs to be in a deep state of relaxation, and it needs to go to sleep. You do not need to 'seek' the vibrational stage that is talked about so often. You absolutely don't need to experience it in order to astral project.

Keep Your Eyes Open

One important tip I give to beginners is that once you're successfully out of your body, don't close your eyes. Keep them open the entire time you explore the astral; there's no need to even blink in the non-physical. Even if you want to transport to another location or dimension, keep your eyes open. Closing your eyes *can* be a method of going back to your physical body. Experienced practitioners are more able to close them without going back to their body, but for novices, it doesn't come as naturally. Your vision in the astral is what keeps you grounded there. However, if you do find yourself out of body with your eyes already closed and struggle to open them; you can try to open them with your (astral) fingertips, and you should then be able to see. If not, your instinct to go back to your physical body may be too strong, be comfortable in being separate from your physical body.

Lack of vision sometimes happens when we first start having experiences because it's like our ordinary waking consciousness is getting used to using an entirely new body; your astral body. The same effect can even happen when walking in your astral body; your legs might feel very heavy; in this case, you could try to use your hands to pick your feet up. It can also be remedied by just sheer willpower. In any case, such effects gradually wear off, and you'll be controlling your astral body in no time, just as a baby eventually learns to walk and talk with their new physical body.

NAVIGATING THE ASTRAL REALM

Once you're out of body, there is no method required to do what you want to do or go where you desire. You simply intend it with the power of your will. Your emotions become your guiding force, your compass. You do this the same way you want to go to your bedroom to sleep or your kitchen to eat - you don't think about it; you simply just get up and go. Let's say you find yourself out of body, and you want to visit Paris, you can simply fly through the sky while intending to arrive in Paris. You won't see yourself flying past the exact physical way there, nor will it take you the same time as it takes for a plane to fly there; you will arrive within moments. You may even see a wormhole effect around you, or everything may just become black for a few seconds until you pop up in your desired location.

In various esoteric teachings, they describe the astral plane as the fifth dimension. Assuming this is correct, we can go off the ground that science states that the fifth dimension is beyond space and time. If the astral plane is beyond space and time, then this is why we are able to transcend physical distances between two points and why we're able to visit the past and future. To visit the past or future, we use the same principle; intention. Intention is your driving wheel, and it's important to note that it is beneficial to have some sort of goal that you would like to fulfil or some kind of location you would like to visit before coming out of body. The astral body is inherently energetic and likes to have a destination. If a vehicle doesn't have a destination, then there's no need for it to stay switched on and it might as well turn itself off to save energy – and in my understanding, astral projection requires a lot of spiritual energy, so use your time wisely, but don't rush. Just set your destination and enjoy the ride. The astral body is more advanced than a self-driving car; don't underestimate it, trust it.

Think of one or two things you would like to do once out of body; they can be as ambitious as visiting a deceased relative, visiting another planet or seeing major events in the past. On the other hand, they can be as simple as analysing a rock, exploring your house or going on a walk down your local street. The important thing is to have a goal in mind because often, we like to overthink the process. When we overthink, we worry or get overexcited; as a result, we lose our focus and go back to the physical body.

It's also important to note that you do not need to complete the goal you had in mind; as you journey into your experience, you may see something that interests you more, or you may feel a burning desire, in-the-moment, to do something else. You could see an event or a carnival you may want to join, or you might suddenly like to enquire about a problem that you want to sort out in your current physical life; in this case, you could simply ask the question either out loud or mentally, and you may even see a 'guide' appear to give you some advice. Alternatively, you can ask for a guide before going to sleep too!

When it comes to language in the astral, you will find that anyone you speak to will usually speak the same language as you. It's not that they necessarily know your country's language intellectually, but that there is some sort of universal auto-translation in the astral that gets the person's communicated messages to us and interprets them in perfect real-time. This sort of communication is absolutely efficient, and you often don't just hear the person in perfect words, but you also understand them, in the complete sense of understanding – in essence, it is telepathy, our base-level of communication on the most human type of interconnectedness. How you interpret these messages also depends on your skill and openness to intuit them.

When you see someone talking to you, you may even see images appear about what they're talking about, and you'll feel the emotions they are feeling. When you experience this directly, you begin to understand how to bridge this power into the physical; it's precisely how clairvoyance and clairaudience works. For example, one time, while I was out of my body, I decided to visit a cinema in the astral plane. I walked inside and sat down in one of the back rows. There were only a few people inside. Instead of being interested in what was on the screen, I glanced over at a man sitting in one of the middle rows. He watched the screen intently, and as I watched him, I saw pictures floating around his head area which were images from his life; I saw his dog, his house, that he smoked cigarettes, I saw his family etc. As I was gazing, soon he turned his head and looked straight at me. I was surprised and got up and left, realising that, unlike the physical, people in the astral seem to be more sensitive to telepathic occurrences - similarly, I know this can be the same case in the physical too; I've had numerous occasions in waking life where I'm looking at a person, and they turn to look at me without any physical prompt. I'm sure you've probably experienced this in physical life too, try it out!

To use a more amusing example of telepathy and 'intuited' language, I've had several occasions where I have spoken to cats. In one excursion, I found myself in a family's home. In the home, the family members were all excited and were celebrating the fact that they were getting some new kittens. However, when I looked at their current adult cat – I could feel that he was not happy. I asked him what was wrong, and he said, in plain English, "I don't like the way humans are; I like you though, you're simple, others should be like that", I was concerned for him and asked specifically why he wasn't happy with them getting kittens, he said "I'm just not happy that they're getting kittens", I asked him why again, but he didn't explain and continued in his solemn mood. On another occasion, while out of body, I was walking down a street when I came across a stray cat. I knew he was a stray simply by looking at him, not his appearance but by naturally intuiting his life. I said hello to him, and again, in plain English, he said hello back. He said to me, "Look at those humans over there", pointing to a group of people across the road. I said, "Yes, what about them?", he said, "Humans are pets, not cats". I asked him what he meant by that, but in the casual way of a typical cat, he turned his back on me, uninterested. I then realised what he meant, amused. He was a stray, and like many strays in neighbourhoods, he probably had a collection of local 'human pets' he would visit to utilise for food and shelter.

So even though sometimes you may hear plain English, it's not always necessary. Still, you can see here how communicating to an animal, who doesn't have the facility to speak human language in the physical, can still convey their communication in a way that suits our own human perception, at least that's how we interpret it.

It can be difficult and takes skill to know where you are and what kind of dimensional plane you're on, whether you're on a higher or lower vibrational dimension. Sometimes it's obvious, and sometimes it's not. You must use your own intuition. Sometimes I find myself amongst other people, and I feel no unease in introducing myself to them because they're either other people unconsciously projecting from their sleep, or 'dead' people who are inhabitants of those dimensions. However, on other occasions, I project to locations where I immediately instinctively feel I should not try to approach or talk to them because I am witnessing something that is taking place in physical reality or because the person feels very hostile, most likely within a lower plane of the astral. Often though, a good indication of whether you're in the higher or lower astral is whether the environment is light or dark, in other words, day or night. Although this isn't a full-proof way to tell, it's a common characteristic that higher planes are usually brighter, and lower planes are often darker.

Another peculiar wonder about these worlds is that animals' non-physical counterparts can often look different from how they appear in the physical. For example, in the physical, when I lived in a property in London, a local cat would often visit me through my window. I've always been fascinated by cats and always strived to learn from their visibly meditative Zen-like state of being - if you would like to live with a Zen master, then get a cat. I decided to befriend him and utilise him for my practices. Around a week after being with him often, I came out of my body. To my surprise, instead of seeing my small regular cat friend, I saw a large black jaguar; I was taken aback and almost felt fear. Still, I knew it was my same little friend as he acted in precisely the same way he does in the physical, with the way he moved around and played, and also by the energy signature I felt from him.

Another example of this that I've seen multiple times is in birds; one time, out of my body, I heard knocking on my bedroom window. I went to see what it was. It was a crow the size of a large dog; it filled my entire window. Other than birds, I have not noticed other types of animals presenting themselves differently. Perhaps this is why birds and cats have been long honoured in various spiritual traditions and cultures throughout history.

Different appearances in the astral can be the case for humans too, but being the complicated beings we are, there are many things to consider when someone has a different appearance in the astral compared to the physical. A person can change their appearance at any given moment by their will or belief of what they look like, or how they feel if they're depressed or happy. We can also occupy several egoic forms of ourselves; for example you could see the angry or happy part of someone. This is why this topic is more complicated when it comes to humans than animals; animals are purer, innocent, and do not have the challenge of belief and intellectualism. Most of the time, though, most of us will assume our regular, usual physical appearance; powered by expectation and habit, it's just what we're used to. Shapeshifting is possible, though, and just like navigating to other locations, you only need intent to do it.

STEP-BY-STEP METHODS

By now, I've made it clear that the best practice is an intuitive and instinctive practice that doesn't wholly rely on a step-by-step method. I've made it clear that astral projection requires no thinking. This doesn't mean we can't think about it or talk about it. It is like when you're practising for your driving license. You have the theory and the practice. You can theorise all you want about driving a car, but when it comes to actually driving it, it's best to clear your mind and feel the car in-the-moment; if thoughts of excessive theory come and interrupt you while you're driving, it may mess with your 'flow', and you might crash. It's important to feel confident, in control and absolutely sure of yourself – and even if you don't feel that way; just 'fake it till you make it' as they say. With this in mind, let's look at some step-by-step methods of the process that I've put together. Towards the end of the book, I will also share a summary of my own personal approach.

Subconscious Method Through Intent

This is one of the easiest and simplest ways to approach astral projection, but it is also a core aspect of any method. You see, it is barely ever your conscious mind which takes you out of your body, but your subconscious. That is, it happens naturally and spontaneously without you having to make a lot of conscious effort. The only effort you need to make is the one with preparing the subconscious through affirmations and meditation. Astral projection can work like any other bodily function, the breath, heart-beating, growing your hair or nails or going to the toilet. They all happen automatically, and so too you can come out of your body automatically. This approach goes back to trusting and believing in yourself and letting go of the idea that you need systematic step-by-step logical methods. When you go to sleep, simply have conviction that your subconscious will take you out of body. We come out of body unconsciously every night, so all that needs to happen is your awareness being placed within the process of it while you sleep. This can happen before, during or after separation – you do not *need* to experience actually leaving the body. As you drift off to sleep at night, you can say to yourself, "I WILL come out of body", and as you go about your day, ask yourself as many times as possible, "Am I in the astral?" whilst at the same time analysing your surroundings meticulously and genuinely curious. You will surely ask this one day when you're unconsciously in the astral plane.

An effective way to solidify intent is to reach a deep state of meditation before sleep; and amidst that profoundly deep state, mentally recite "I WILL astral project" and sense your expectation that it WILL happen as you fall to sleep. The more profound of a state that you are in while you say it, the more effective it will be. Think of deep meditation as digging a hole into your subconscious; the deeper you go, the deeper you can plant a seed of intention for it to take life and autonomously manifest your desired results.

WBTB Method Through Sleep

I have found it best to practise this method after anywhere between four to six hours of sleep. Deciding on how many hours into your sleep you wake up is entirely up to you. Follow your instincts; you need to feel well-rested and peaceful enough to get up and practice, but at the same time, you need to feel lethargic enough to quickly fall back to sleep. Also, consider how much time you have before having to wake up for the day's duties. Going back to sleep with having to wake up one hour later isn't the most effective approach. The thought of having to wake up so soon can be distracting; the activities of the day will soon be knocking at your subconscious. Instead, find a time that is peaceful for you. If you have pets, who love to jump on you at any moment's notice, keep them out of the room. But if they are well behaved, and you find their presence next to you relaxing, it is no problem.

When you get up in the middle of your sleep, you can also go to another location, perhaps your sofa or another bed, which is only for coming out of body. This can help your subconscious remember your intent and familiarise this location with the habitual energy of your spiritual practice. However, this isn't completely necessary. Personally, I have had most of my experiences while in my regular bed sleeping next to my wife. However, if you're very determined, a separate room dedicated to this practice can help a lot; having your own psychic space to focus in is beneficial.

Similarly, it does not matter what position you are in; I have personally come out of my body in almost every position. However, I find laying on my back is best for focus, but if you can't fall asleep in this position, don't worry; sleeping in another position is fine. What's important is that you are relaxed enough to fall asleep. Relaxation of our muscles goes a lot deeper than most of us think. An interesting fact I came across is that some 'Relaxology' sources will tell you that the muscles of your jaw can be relaxed so profoundly that your jaw actually has the ability to hang loosely from your skull, instead of its usual tense disposition. Try to relax your own jaw in this way; you'll see it's not something achievable in an instant - so make the effort to practice deep relaxation in every part of your body before any practice.

Exercise 7: Separating Upon Sleep

1. Find a comfortable and quiet place to lay down.
2. Begin by visualising or feeling a warm golden light entering your body through your feet. Relax and let go of your feet and go upwards, feeling the same relaxing light penetrate every cell of your body, through your legs, groin, stomach, organs, chest, shoulders, arms, hands, throat, face, eyes, jaw, head, ears. Let go of every muscle and surrender.
3. Affirm to yourself, "I will wake up in my sleep into a lucid dream (or astral projection)". With this affirmation, *feel* deep within you that you *will* wake up in the middle of your sleep. You must be sure of it, confident, expect it and trust your subconscious to wake you up. If you doubt it, it won't happen. If you believe it, it will happen. You can also just set an alarm for this, but you will find with practice, using intention to wake up at specific times actually works. This can be a great way to understand how we can effectively rely on our own intent for astral projection too.
4. Fall asleep, relaxed and well-rested. There is no need for any special practice here. Don't fill your mind with stress; feel your comfortable body and fall asleep peacefully like a cat or baby. There is no stress here—no need for your mind to wander about what to do next. Be rested.
5. If and when you wake up in the middle of the night, naturally, you'll feel uncoordinated since your consciousness has most likely been roaming around aimlessly as it usually does during the sleep of the physical body. Immediately remember where you are and remember your intent. You can get up, go to sleep in another location, or stay where you are, but get up out of bed and move a little. At the same time, maintain your 'drowsiness'; this feeling of sleepiness is essential to maintain so that you can easily fall back to sleep.

6. When you get back into bed, repeat the affirmation in step three and follow the same relaxation process. However, instead of just sleeping to sleep, this time, aim to stay conscious during the precise moment between wakefulness and sleep. To do this, observe yourself, your mind, your feelings, your sleepiness, notice your body drifting away. Remember that you are not your body; you are not your mind. Optionally, you can repeat to yourself as you sleep, "Mind awake, body asleep".
7. At the transition between wakefulness and sleep, in that all encumbering sleepiness where you're so tempted to just fall into unconsciousness, suddenly use forceful willpower to get up out of your body. You may induce a feeling of vibrations through this; this is a good sign that you will shortly be able to lean into those sensations and get up out of body. However, do not tense the physical body in any way.

Direct Method Through Meditation

This is the most advanced method; the previous two methods are more to do with tricking your mind and taking advantage of the moment of sleep. However, this method is the one that will enable you to fully comprehend the entire process deeply; beyond descriptions or intellectual analysis, you will *know* it within a profound level of your awareness. You will understand every step and be able to teach others as I am teaching you. However, this method can take months, if not years to master, and it is much better to let go of any expectation for success with it in the short term. It is a long-term goal that will happen naturally. Besides, the point of deep meditation is to have no goal. Thus, it is futile to meditate in order to attain an 'astral projection' state – the astral projection state occurs paradoxically without *wanting* it, through transcending unconscious layers of the mind.

It is better to adopt daily meditation and just know that one day, during a meditation session, it could happen. Meditate for the sake of awakening consciousness, don't tirelessly 'seek' experiences, for that would be counterproductive against proper meditation of being in a detached state of being. This is a paradox, but this is how it works.

Exercise 8: Tips for Daily Deep Meditation with the Potential for Astral Projection

1. Focusing on coming out of the body defeats the purpose of meditation. The objective is to go beyond all thoughts, all desire, all sense-perceptions. The mind thinks that it needs to *do* something in order to astral project. The fact of the matter is that we need to exit the mind altogether and enter our spatial state of consciousness. And to do this, we go beyond it by simply observing it for extended periods of time. And by just observing it, without adding more judgements or agitations, we come to the direct realisation that we are not our minds and that it is making noise completely by itself. We realise that we are that which is observing; you are the observer of experience, not the observed. Realising this, we can detach ourselves from the limitations of the mind with all its habitual ways of *wanting* to solve problems through analysing and overthinking. Thus, if you are diligent, you will begin to experience genuine peace. But it doesn't just stop there. Continue profoundly into this state, and you will find that as you become experienced in *being* the *observer*, you will realise that you have freedom, in the sense that your awareness is not limited by your body. Thus, coming out of the body is a natural ability. You will realise you never had to think about anything in order to project – all you had to do was 'undo' and let go.

2. In the midst of deep meditation, especially if you practice for at least twenty minutes or so, you may notice you start to see vivid scenes in your perception - this is a completely normal part of the process; it's like seeing your thoughts, but they are becoming more subconscious, just don't follow them and don't let them distract you from your well-maintained practice. You see, the mind successfully distracts us all the time with its usual ways, but when it sees that simple thoughts aren't working, it will begin to present visual scenes to you, and there will be a sensation of temptation to follow them. Don't be tempted, simply recognise them as distractions and continue your practice of impartialness and neutrality and don't identify or attach with them. Remember that astral projection is not about thinking, imagination, visualisation, dreaming or even visions. Astral projection is free from all imaginings. You'll absolutely know this when you experience it.
3. Eventually, as you meditate and go beyond all the forms and objects in your consciousness, there will come a point amongst the quietude of nothingness, like the cracking of a shell, where you will find yourself in another reality. It will just happen. Your usual ordinary worldly perceptual barriers will give way from the force and strength of your spiritual disposition. I know this last part does not sound very descriptive, but this is genuinely how it can happen. It can occur by grace or without knowing. There can even be a moment of unconsciousness, and when you bring yourself back by the strength of your habitual practice, you may find yourself in another reality. Other than this, you may also experience the vibrational or hypnagogic state where you can lean into it and leave the body, but as I've mentioned, don't 'look' or 'try' to induce this state. Additionally, you may also enter 'conscious sleep' where you are aware of your

surroundings, but at the same time, your body enters a sort of superior type of sleep, much like how cats sleep - and since you're asleep, you can naturally leave the body. In Yoga Nidra, they teach sleep meditation, which is to reach a state between being awake and sleeping. You can also look into Shabd Yoga, which instructs on how to 'listen to the inner sound', which naturally leads to out of body experiences.

DIFFERENT DIMENSIONS OF THE ASTRAL

The astral plane is multidimensional, and with that, we have the whole spectrum of human emotions reflected in these non-physical dimensions. The reality of the lower astral is here and now. Many very low vibrational and persistently depressed people are already living in the lower astral within themselves even though they still have a physical body. It is an easy and straightforward dimension to overcome, of course, though it's not that easy if you ask the people living in those states of consciousness. We all have our challenges and self-limiting beliefs, which keep us anchored in certain states of consciousness. A lot of it comes down to a lack of self-worth, guilt, fear or other related emotions. What's more is, if one continues being in this state of consciousness and their physical body dies, then they won't really experience anything that different in their afterlife. Thus, our concepts of 'hell' and 'heaven' are applicable to our state of consciousness here and now – not in the future when death comes our way.

So, just as there is a spectrum from lower to higher human emotions, so too is there a spectrum of astral dimensions of lower, middle and higher planes. The middle part of the astral is mostly Earth-like or parallel to the physical plane. The higher astral are those planes that reflect 'superior' and positive emotions; they are usually beautiful and sunny places, in contrast to the dark regions of the lower astral.

Beyond 'Astral Plane', we find the 'Mental Plane'. This is not something we will explore here. Once you have become grounded and found your way and momentum in meditation and astral travel, you will at times naturally begin to gravitate towards the reality of the mental plane. The 'Mental Plane' is challenging to talk about without doing it injustice. It is a place that is usually free from familiar physical forms as we know it, as it's more to do with the pure energy we feel there.

Our physical world is known as the third dimension, where we are limited in nature by time and space. The 'Astral' is known as the fifth dimension, and the sixth dimension is known as the 'Mental', which is beyond the limitations of the fifth dimension, logically. The Mental plane is not a place where one is subjected to choose from certain lower or higher Astral worlds, but it's actually a dimension that is made up of a sort of superior dimensional energetic unity of all Astral worlds; in a sense, it is the source of all possibilities and realities - all of our emotions synthesised into one all-encompassing intelligence. Understandably, it is beyond duality, beyond good and evil. There are even more dimensions beyond the sixth. However, they are so sublime and so subtle, and so out of intellectual comprehension that to even begin to *think* about them, we would only start to have the capacity to relate them towards the abstract reality of what many call 'God', a divine intelligence beyond anything we could ever even wish to visualise or conceptualise.

BE FEARLESS

If you're feeling fear about astral projection, you need to address it with self-reflection directly. Be aware of it; accept it, but don't fight it. Feeling fear is a natural part of looking into the unknown, but giving in to fear or being overwhelmed by it will increase your chances of having a negative experience.

Fear is like standing at the edge of a cliff looking down at the dark abyss of a canyon; you don't know what lies at the bottom, but you know you have to jump if you want to find out. Be rational and realise that fear is not rational nor useful. After all, your mind cannot imagine what it hasn't even experienced yet; so, don't let it wander or doubt. Centre yourself, focus and breathe – just jump.

"A man goes to knowledge as he goes to war: wide-awake, with fear, with respect, and with absolute assurance. Going to knowledge or going to war in any other manner is a mistake. Forget the self, and you will fear nothing, in whatever level or awareness you find yourself to be."

- *Don Juan Matus (Carlos Castaneda)*

The above quote is an important point if you're a very rationally fearful person; stop indulging in compulsive thoughts about fear-based things you've read or from the tendency of your mind to be paranoid or superstitious; astral projection is a science as well as it is an art. When we experience and comprehend it fully, we realise it is completely logical and rational phenomena, not something otherworldly or scary. Forget yourself, your egos, and focus. As with whatever that you want to achieve in life, don't let anything disturb you from what you initially set out to do.

There's No Such Thing as a Negative Experience

Now, of course, there *are* 'negative experiences', but they only exist subjectively; if we're objective, then the experience only 'is', and that's all. You'll hear of some people having negative experiences in the astral, but more often than not, they are the ones who have interpreted it as such or attracted it to themselves in some way through fear, anxiety or misunderstanding. In the physical, we often interpret experiences subjectively as positive or negative. In a similar way, we interpret our experiences in the astral like this too. In the astral, every thought and emotion can be felt almost instantly; simply put, if you're feeling fear, you will attract fear. Likewise, if you're feeling joy, you will attract joy.

Today, much of collective consciousness in the world is stuck in two-dimensional thinking about what is good and bad, without thinking deeply about what both are, which are actually one and the same. As with most things in life, you will find that there are good things to be found in the bad, and there are bad things to be found in the good. Separation and duality are an illusion. To deny that which is 'evil' is also to deny a part of yourself.

> "It is evil which makes possible the recognition of virtue. To the degree that you condemn and find evil in others, you are to that degree unconscious of the same thing in yourself."
>
> \- *Alan Watts*

The first thing we can do is accept that evil is not separate from us; it is an integral part of our consciousness. In fact, Gnostics believe that about 97% of our consciousness is in an unconscious state, and that most of us on average are only around 3% conscious; that's an idea of the enormity of how much we can awaken to. 97% of us is trapped in darkness, subjectivity or ego, and ultimately this significant part of ourselves is not really that much different from what we call 'evil'. Thus, we often interpret experiences of these states as 'scary', but really, it's just due to our lack of understanding.

The deepest parts of our psyche hold all the secrets to which we do not yet realise. The unconscious is the part of us that our small flames of conscious awareness do not shine through yet; the dimensions inside that need the most love, attention, and comprehension. Therefore, we must change our attitude towards our understanding of evil; without darkness, we wouldn't be able to grow spiritually. Helping others also helps us to understand darkness, as we are ultimately helping ourselves by making better use of our time instead of becoming too self-involved with our egos.

'Heaven' and 'hell' are better described as higher or lower dimensions of the astral, in other words, higher and lower dimensions of consciousness; there isn't just 'one heaven' or 'one hell', but a plethora of complex dimensional levels in-between. The residents of each level are all dependant on their level of consciousness. Higher dimensions are less dense, less dominated by negative emotions. People here are usually happier, having fun, feeling emotions of unconditional love and joy. Whereas lower dimensions are denser, and depending on how deep you go, you'll see people suffering, often because they can't let go of some sort of negativity, attachment, or they harbour some kind of anger, bitterness or regret.

Exploring Lower Realms

The lower astral worlds are, in fact, insightful places we can visit, and if we proceed into them mindfully, there is much wisdom to be gained there. As long as you are detached, objective and approach them with unconditional love for all sentient beings, you will feel safe and keep your wits about you. Remember that nothing dangerous can happen to you, and you can go back to your body whenever you want just by thinking about it. Even crossing a busy road in the physical is more dangerous than astral projection!

While in these lower worlds, you may find you can potentially save a suffering soul from their misery by simply conversing with them out of compassion. As you speak to them and offer them counsel, their appearance may become more attractive, and their surroundings could gradually shift into a higher dimension; this is only if they come to profound realisations about themselves while you talk to them, or perhaps they're simply able to let go of negativity by being able to just talk with someone. Lost souls can only save themselves, but occasionally they can go the right way if we show them the direction.

Gnostics believe Dante, from 'Dante's Inferno', did actually visit the astral, and explored these lower realms. He did so not out of fear or entertainment, but for the purpose of understanding and illuminating these worlds and how they tie to ourselves. You can read about his 'Nine Circles of Hell' which are a glimpse into the mysteries of the lower astral.

Imagine you successfully astral project, but you find yourself in a low dimensional astral world. You may find yourself in a hellish-looking, sinister and hostile realm. Will you interpret this subjectively and run away out of fear, or will you be objective and maintain a detached and calm state where you are in complete assurance that nothing bad can happen to you? The latter is where you should be deeply ingrained. Sometimes we're sent to these lower regions to help someone or learn something new. If you find yourself in such places, be mindful and don't immediately assume you're having some strange 'demonic' experience like what you see in some stereotypical horror movie. In rare cases of individuals who successfully astral project but describe entities attacking them every time they project, my advice is to stop; you're probably not ready, for now. Instead, focus on your physical life and meditate profoundly. Be intelligent and psychologically comprehend your suffering; purify yourself, find happiness, peace and positive emotions. Entities can't feed off our energy if our consciousness is in a higher state of superior feelings of love, peace and bliss! As discussed already – be fearless!

> "Soon you will be where your own eyes will see the source and cause of your miseries and give you their own answer to the mystery."
>
> - *Dante's Inferno*

My interpretation of the above quote is that Dante means sooner or later, whether in meditation, astral projection or our afterlife, we'll see the stark reality of our different sufferings more clearly than we ever have, through which we have the opportunity to comprehend them, and if not, then naturally we will continue to suffer, until we learn. Therefore, we need to deal with our problems here and now; doing so can also prevent harmful things manifesting in the physical, such as relationship issues, business problems, bad health etc. Suffering is part of the human experience. If we want to advance on our path to conscious astral projections in higher dimensions, or heavenly realms, we need to approach this aspect head-on. As above, so below; if we want to perceive objective reality, then we first have to perceive ourselves objectively – this starts with sincere and honest self-reflection.

"When one does not work in the dissolution of the ego, one commits mistakes, and, naturally, these will most likely be committed daily. Thus, mistakes bring problems, and problems bring confusion. Nevertheless, if one works on oneself, everything will march better, because one will advance by eliminating psychological defects."

- *Samael Aun Weor*

One experience I had in the lower astral was witnessing people who were so 'far gone' in their suffering that they appeared as sort of 'zombies'.

Ascending to an Oceanic Planet

12th January 2021

During the depths of a dream, I'm with a group of friends hanging out in a jazz bar. It's a low-key small room with many friendly, relaxed people enjoying music from an improvisation band. I go to the bar and buy some deliciously sliced wagyu beef, served on a paper plate with a toothpick to eat the meat with. We all leave the jazz bar, and I follow behind while enjoying the food.

This dream is nothing out of the ordinary, but eventually I enter the astral plane and what happens next is one of the most dramatic 'shifts' from a lower dimension to a higher dimension that I've ever had.

As I'm walking on the city streets, I lose sight of my friends, and I look for them down dark alleys. The roads seem to become eerier and more desolate. The feeling of fear jolted me into lucidity – this often happens when I feel fear in dreams like my subconscious suddenly switches into high alert and swiftly turns on my waking consciousness to defend itself. Immediately upon realising it's a dream, I become hyper-aware. Not wanting to be in this dream anymore, I intend to stop the dream and enter the astral. However, instead of expecting the dream to collapse and enter a normal Earth-like realm in the astral like I usually do, I involuntarily enter into the lower regions of the astral world.

Instead of being in dark city streets of black and grey like my dream was, I was now in a crumbling post-apocalyptic city of smoky black and red. There was a prominent presence of hostility and insidiousness in the air. I walked down a street, not impressed at all by what I was seeing. Every block of cement had some sort of damage, and small fires were scattered around inside half-demolished buildings causing black smoke to fill the air, and the sky was pitch black with streamy dark grey clouds across its expanse. As I walked around a corner, I saw a big open courtyard, with diseased-looking people everywhere, walking slowly and creepily, clearly with no clue as to where they were going. I thought to myself that I always thought typical Hollywood films of 'zombies' were just an over-exaggerated reflection of the lower worlds, yet here I was watching something that could easily be on the set of 'The Walking Dead'.

To my surprise, I didn't feel much fear, I've met negative lower beings before who have been more terrifying, and these 'zombies' appeared to be so feeble-minded that they didn't seem like much of a threat. I even considered if I could help these people who were unquestionably lost souls. I watched them for a few moments, looking for any sign of intelligence when one seemed to noticed me. His face, arms, hands and legs had blood, rashes and scars all over them, and his skin had a tint of grey as if he was ill to the bone. His clothes were ragged, dirty and shredded. As I looked into his eyes, I saw barely any glimpse of life, perhaps deep inside, I saw fear, but there was a strong feeling of anger and malice on the surface. What must this person have gone through to get to such a state? Perhaps years of drug abuse and addiction did this to him. He looked at me for a few moments, and I considered whether I would be able to talk to him; he took a few steps towards me and then suddenly began running at me with a treacherous growl. As he got within an inch of me, without any thought, I cast a force of light at him, which threw him backwards and into the air. I'd never done this before; it was instinctive. I watched him fall and get back up. Realising that there wasn't much I could do here, I intended to leave this place, and I felt myself travelling downwards underground; I began to hear a demonic voice and realised I was going in the wrong direction! With pure willpower, I forcefully flew upwards and chanted the mantra "OM", and I flew back up through the surface, leaving the crowd of diseased humans beneath me. The fear of going even lower than that dimension and hearing that evil voice frightened me and, in turn, must have given me such a powerful surge of energy because the next part blew my mind.

As I chanted "OM" and flew upwards, ascending through dimensions, I didn't just stop and arrive somewhere normal as I usually do. Instead, I accelerated even faster, and I felt myself enter through what I can only describe as penetrating a celestial atmosphere. If the Earth's atmosphere is the Earth's head, I felt my head and mind expand as if my consciousness was merging into space. I felt myself lose my usual form and became only awareness. I enjoyed this expanding feeling so much that I willed myself to go even faster, and I soon seemed to be travelling through a wormhole. I intended to go far into space and beyond the stars as I possibly could. I began to see stars, planets, meteors and space clouds go past me; I knew that in a sense I was flying past them at a breakneck speed, but in another sense, it also felt like the objects were going past me, rather than me just travelling past them. Wormhole travel must genuinely be to do with bending the laws of space, time and distance to get somewhere faster instead of just travelling in the physical sense of "A to B".

As if by magic, I eventually found myself inside the room of a tall building filled with bright light. I looked at my hands; I was back in my usual form. The room I was in gave the impression of a hotel, it was immaculate, and all the furniture was pure white. I was standing in front of a tall and wide floor-length window, looking out at the most majestic vastness of crystal-clear ocean I'd ever seen. There was pure golden light on the sky's horizon, and the atmosphere dispersed upwards to the top of the sky into a glowing neon blue gradient. There was an island in the middle of the ocean with colourful tropical-like vegetation that was not familiar to me. What caught my attention next was looking below the sea; there were giant sea creatures the size of whales swimming in groups. They looked like a mixture between a whale, goldfish and koi at the same time. There were people on the water, or humanoids for a better word, not exactly human, but they had the same structure as humans, except they looked larger, more flexible and less hairy, and they were clearly good swimmers. I considered whether this was some form of 'oceanic humanoid species' on a planet unknown to humanity. I've had no prior knowledge about such a species, nor any interest in such things, yet here I was. Why did my consciousness bring me here? I was trying to discern them, but the problem was I was so high up in the building so I couldn't distinguish them clearly. I felt that I was so far from Earth that I was the one who felt like an alien, and I felt like I had to conceal myself; I felt reluctant to get closer in fear of drawing attention to myself. On the other hand, these people looked incredibly joyous and friendly. Some of them were riding on boat-like vehicles. Most of them were swimming or standing on platforms above the water. Even though I could barely see them, I could see they were enjoying themselves profusely, jumping in and out of the sea, riding in boats with their arms in the air and swimming with the sea creatures. I could hear their cheering and laughter. I couldn't help but smile in awe of them. They enjoyed swimming with the animals, and they unquestionably had a close bond with them. The joy they were radiating was immense and infectious; I felt so ecstatic that I wanted to fly to them and join them. I watched the giant fish swimming under the water and jumping into the air and playing with the people. They were all carefree and happy; it was a stark contrast to where I had just been.

The fact that I was in a hotel-like building with people having all sorts of water-based fun made me feel like I was on a planet where happiness and leisure were a usual way of life; it felt remarkably light compared to our dense world on Earth. I looked around my bare white room. I saw a holographic screen on a wall, which had my location on a map; I didn't recognise the landscape, most of it was water, which made me consider it was probably mostly a water-based planet.

The feeling of being on another planet became even stronger when I saw their moon in the sky – it was no regular moon; it was bigger and shining powerfully, as bright as a star! It looked as if it had solar rays beaming from its sides. I was baffled, and as I stared into the moon, trying to figure out how it was so bright, I started to feel off-balance. At this point, there was someone in the room with me; I heard a female voice tell me about the place. I couldn't make out her appearance; I told the woman I had to go as I felt myself losing energy. Even though I couldn't see her, I could feel her smiling at me; I felt love.

I let myself go. My awareness gracefully glided back to my body, and I felt my physical presence again; I didn't move or open my eyes and recollected the entire experience, all the way from when I was in a dream in the jazz bar. Whilst recalling, I had a deep sense that I had been to that planet before. I knew the woman in the room with me; maybe I had a past life there, I'm not sure. Maybe that's the reason I went there out of anywhere else; after feeling a jolt of fear in the lower regions of the astral, perhaps a deep part of me wanted to go somewhere familiar, somewhere happy.

One thing that confused me the most was the moon shining like a star. It made me consider whether I was in the third-dimensional world or not. I'm not sure whether it's scientifically possible for a moon to shine so brightly. Maybe their star was very close, and the moon reflected more powerfully as a result, or perhaps I was in a much higher dimensional plane than I thought, where such things are possible. It also reminded me about esoteric texts I've read that point towards both moons and water being representations of emotion, which relates to how the species I saw were highly and positively emotional water-based spirits.

Thus, this is just one example of how we can gain interesting experiences in the lower astral, and, instead of acting out of fear, we can calmly proceed to more profound levels of reality.

RECAP: THERE'S NO ULTIMATE METHOD

The ultimate method is not following a method, but going with the flow of your natural and intelligent instincts. Instead of thinking about steps, the ultimate method is to *be* in a state of consciousness already that is ideal for astral projection. That is, to naturally intend and be receptive enough to become aware of whatever phenomena presents itself to you during the stages of sleep.

Why is there no definitive method? Well, if there was, we would see a lot more astral projectors in the world, wouldn't we? Ultimately the practice is an art that has to be refined with time, you have to put in the work, and you will reap the benefits. Astral projection is absolutely natural and organic. It is part of our *Being*. You already know how to do it; you just need to re-discover it for yourself first-hand, and once you do, it will become easier. I'm not going to excessively add to already hundreds of techniques out there; if you wish to follow one, then do it, but the purpose of this book has been to guide you on connecting with your more profound and long-term approach through contemplation and intuition. Let your heart always be the undercurrent of your approach and understanding, and take note that one day you will not need these 'stepping stone guides' to achieve it, they are like having stabilisers on your bike, one day you will know how to ride the bike without them.

This should be a relief to know, especially for those who have been placing their absolute trust in 'promising' step-by-step methods but have only experienced disappointment through having no success with them. Techniques can encourage too much thinking and expectation, and this often gets in the way of getting into the natural flow of things. Stress is the opposite state of consciousness that you want to inhabit in order to astral project. Relaxation and inspired emotions will always be superior for the astral traveller.

Remember, astral projection is synonymous with the awakening of consciousness – the awakening of consciousness is synonymous with the death and transcendence of the ego – the transcendence of the ego is synonymous with staying intensely in the eternal realm of the present moment – and staying present is synonymous with direct access to the creative realm and spontaneous energy that is essential for astral projection – this is also all synonymous with self-healing and self-knowledge. Hence is the path.

It is necessary to know that humanity lives with its consciousness primarily asleep. People work asleep. People walk through the streets asleep. People live and die asleep. When we see and understand that the entire world lives asleep, including ourselves, we comprehend the necessity of awakening. We need the awakening of consciousness. We need to want the awakening of consciousness. We are asleep and dreaming from moment to moment, look around the room and see where you are in right now - are you dreaming? Are you really looking and intensely asking the question?

We need to unlearn what we have learned from society, parents, friends and schools. Empty your cup and clean your windows of perception and truly see without mind, without labels, without the human filter of artificial judgement and interpretation. Connect with the root of your purest inner nature.

How can you expect to see or experience the spiritual realm of the astral if you are daydreaming in your daily life? Be awake in the day, and you will be awake in the night. As above, so below.

My personal message is that if you genuinely want to experience the reality of the astral in its depths, you must commit to working on the awakening of consciousness every day, not just for yourself but for others. Accordingly, you will experience the joy of working on becoming *human*, for what other way is there to live? Astral projection is about living and realising life itself. It is a transcendental and joyous way to live.

There are laws in the astral, just as there is in the physical. Suppose you are under the influence of a particular ego, such as always being angry. In that case, your psychological state will not allow you into certain peaceful places in the astral, and perhaps not as many guides will respond to you. This is just one example of such a law. It is karma; every state of being has a consequence.

As another example, if you are very lustful and you see an attractive woman or man, you may chase them in the astral out of impulse, and as a consequence, you will lose your lucidity, your consciousness; why? Because you have lost control, you are instead controlled by your impulses. This is why mindfulness, self-control and self-knowledge must be exercised.

So, the principles given in this book may not promise a direct technique to astral projection. Still, I promise you it is the only one worthwhile, and it applies to every single technique out there. If you work on yourself, you'll eventually have astral projection experiences which are naturally longer and more profound. This is the real art and practice of astral projection; the experience is given to you by grace when you put in the real human work – not by following simple step-by-step experiments as a half-hearted curious individual. Astral projection is the direct experience of the soul, and thus it should be upheld and honoured in such a way!

So, try to make time for at least ten minutes a day of daily meditation of letting go, relaxation and surrender, to begin with. Add another ten minutes if you had a tough day. Analyse and comprehend whatever ego you can identify, whether it be anger, laziness, depression, anxiety etc. Analyse the stories you are telling yourself, don't speak to yourself when doing this. You only need silent awareness; the soundless wisdom of the heart will guide you. Learn to listen to this quiet inner intelligence. You will feel whether the stories you tell yourself are needed or not. If not, then let go of them.

Let go of any various self-limiting beliefs that imply you can only astral project through methods. Any experienced person knows that it can happen naturally and spontaneously, even when you go to sleep without any intentions.

Furthermore, deep relaxation is essential; denying yourself and working on your egos can cause tension or stress. It's like a chick trying to break out of its shell. In the long term, it's like the caterpillar metamorphosing into a butterfly. It all takes conscious effort and growth to get to this flowering stage of non-physical experience. Accordingly, be gentle with yourself; there is never any need to strain yourself.

Our minds have been conditioned to follow manuals and guides for everything. Little in society teaches us to follow our feelings, intuition, instinct, heart, creativity, conscience, or thrive off inspiration.

- Say affirmations every night that you will astral project and/or become lucid in your dreams.
- Wake up at least once every middle of the night to reset your intentions and go back to sleep.
- Recall your experiences every morning.

Even just committing yourself to the few points above will provide results; the problem is that most people just lack the willpower to carry them out. Perhaps some days you will say to yourself, "I'm just so unsure on my next steps" – don't worry, the mind is always looking for the next thing to do. Yet astral projection requires the mind to be still. Astral projection is a state of surrender, of letting go, of literally getting out of our minds. *Feel* that you already have everything that you need; and it will be given to you.

There is also the phenomena of 'sleep paralysis', I have not touched on this in-depth because you simply do not *need* to experience it nor induce it. However, if you're in true sleep paralysis, you should be able to just simply 'get up' out of your body; this requires no thinking, just do it. It is usually much easier to leave the body in this state, because the physical body is simply paralysed, allowing awareness to freely roam as long as it is not encumbered with the belief that it has to be attached to the physical body. Some people get stuck in this state because they feel fear, but if they simply stop indulging in fear, they will see that they can simply use their *will* to separate from the physical body.

Perhaps you begin to experience boredom while attempting to astral project, or whilst your meditating – in that case, you only need to become aware of boredom itself; do not identify with it, detach yourself. Be aware and accept whatever state you ever find yourself in. What you accept, you go beyond. This is how we transcend any state and go deeper into more profound levels of reality.

The ultimate method to astral project is; the spiritual one. It may not be the fastest one, but it is the most powerful one and the only one that is most worthwhile, for now and after death.

Now with all that said, let me present to you the following step-by-step method. You could call this a simplified summary of my own approach towards astral projection. I hope you find it helpful:

1. Be interested and passionate, read books, meditate, and watch videos on astral projection, study it and

contemplate it in much of your free time.

2. ALWAYS question your reality as often as you can. Ask yourself throughout the day, "Am I in the Astral?"... do reality checks to confirm. My favourite reality check is; hold your nostrils shut and try to breathe through them; if you can't, then you're in the physical. If you can, then you're in a dream. If you're in a dream, try flying or falling to induce vibrations to enter the Astral plane (as discussed in 'Exercise 5').
3. Before sleeping, intend to wake up in the middle of the night or set an alarm for you to get up and go back to sleep anywhere between four and six hours of sleep. This will act as a second attempt and give a jolt to your consciousness to boost your REM cycle. When you wake up in the middle of your sleep, simply walk around for a bit, or meditate, stay feeling drowsy so that you can easily fall back to sleep.
4. As you drift to sleep (both when you first go to sleep AND after you wake up in the middle of the night), say affirmations such as, "I WILL Astral Project, I WILL be conscious while my physical body sleeps, I WILL travel to where I intend to go". You must feel this EMOTIONALLY, feel it in your body, desire it, crave it, WILL it. Do not say it robotically; believe every word wholeheartedly as if you are praying.
5. Alternatively, if you are comfortable with mentally reciting mantras as you sleep; I was taught by my Gnostic teacher these two mantras, which I have had much success with: "FA RA ON" and "LA RA S" - lull yourself to sleep with one of these. Without knowing how, you will spontaneously find yourself in the Astral plane at some point during sleep. They are pronounced; "FFFFAAAA... RRRRAAAA... OOOONNNN" and

"LLLLAAAA.... RRRRAAAA.... SSSSS" (separated by a breath between each syllable).

6. Either as you fall to sleep or in the middle of sleep, you may begin to feel vibrations, DO NOT panic or get over-excited. Be like a Zen monk; go with the flow, remember your goal. You will eventually be able to simply WILL yourself out of your body, to simply get up or float up, or intend to stand in a location in your room.
7. Once you're out, DO NOT overthink anything, remain like a Zen monk and just get outside your house; that is your mission. Carry out your will, your desire. Achieve what you set out to do. Or, if you had no prior intent, simply just walk - explore and appreciate your surroundings; visual appreciation keeps you grounded. The Astral plane is VISION of LIGHT after all; your third eye is active in varying degrees in these moments, visually and peripherally take in the environment! Don't forget to breathe and stay calm. Enjoy your experience.
8. When you wake up, don't move; replay the entire experience in your memory in detail, then write it all down or record it as a voice memo. If you didn't Astral project, you must still record ALL of your dreams, no matter how insignificant you think they are. Every dream and every detail you manage to recall, the stronger you enforce your connection to the non-physical dimension and memory of it, massively boosting your chances of Astral projection in the future.
9. Above all - if nothing happens, that is FINE! Every attempt is progress, whether on a conscious or unconscious level. Your subconscious learns no matter what, success or not. You have to be patient; this is crucial. We sleep every day, which means you have every day to practice. The average lifespan is 70+ years old;

there are 25550 days in 70 years, so you have at least 25550 attempts. Every night you don't do it is a night wasted; what else will you do when you go to sleep? Nothing. You might as well Astral project and make better use of your time. If you are truly patient and have faith that you WILL eventually Astral project, I guarantee it will happen.

Also, if you're wondering about how long it will take for you to achieve the out of body state, and you keeping asking yourself when it will happen - it's less about how quick it can happen and more about one's skill to reach a level of consciousness whereby astral projection flows naturally.

In such a state, one would never ask or wonder how long it takes because such a question implies that one is trying to reach a particular state. Yet, the state of mind of the astral projector only reaches their 'astral state' through allowing and accepting whatever state they are already in.

So, since we're all infinitely unique, there is no definitive time that it takes to achieve astral projection; it entirely depends on the individual. The point is, this is nothing to worry or think about; all you need to do is practice, and in your practice, you will likely find yourself in states of consciousness where your mind does not ask such a question, so stay in the frame of mind and unwearyingly wait for your experience to unfold.

HARNESSING SEXUAL ENERGY

This is an additional part I would like to include, for I feel it is important. The primal force of sexual energy is essential to talk about because many people simply just don't have enough energy to maintain awareness during out of body experiences to begin with. Furthermore, this type of energy cannot just be ignored; it is a part of our nature after all. Sexual energy can be a great source of energy. Many of us don't even have enough energy to maintain attention during our waking lives, never mind while we're asleep. This is where harnessing sexual energy can be beneficial.

Just as the human being, along with its microcosmic world, is born through sex, so too is the macrocosmic universe. There is power in this energy, but we often overlook its potential because we only direct it towards, and understand it as, the human sexual act. However, it is an energy that permeates all of creation. Most people think it is only solely used for procreation, but this couldn't be further from the truth. Creating a baby is only one purpose of sexual energy; it can create a person externally, yes, but it can also give us the force to create ourselves anew, internally. It *can* be used as a tool for personal transformation.

I am not saying sex is bad or negative; no, it is a natural and sacred part of our nature, best enjoyed through love. However, when too much of this energy is focused merely on physical sex, lust, desires, passions, etc., it can drain us of energy through the unconsciousness of impulse. On the other hand, when we are mindful and don't excessively use it in that way, we can instead use that energy to direct and transform it into other creative outlets - in astral projection, it can strengthen our intent and willpower, improving our memory and focus in non-physical states.

We have our intellect, instincts, and emotions, but sexual energy is an even deeper part of ourselves that is commonly overlooked, misunderstood and misused. Utilising it in the correct way for our practice can have clarifying and rejuvenating effects.

Ultimately, harnessing sexual energy is really about saving energy. Most of us simply don't have enough energy to spend on what we want; everyone these days is tired, and there are endless adverts and new products out there promising to give you more energy. But when we start to get a grip of our excessive thoughts, emotions and sexual desires, we begin to save energy. This newfound energy source can then be better utilised for the things we want to manifest in life, in this case, spiritual realisation and astral projection.

"A warrior has nothing in the world except his or her impeccability. Impeccability is defined as being perfect or having no flaws; incapable of wrongdoing. However, in the [spiritual] warrior sense, impeccability is to save or conserve energy. Impeccability is nothing else but the proper use of energy. This statement has no inkling of morality. When we have saved energy, that makes us impeccable. To understand this, we have to save enough energy ourselves."

- *Don Juan Matus (Carlos Castaneda)*

If you think your thoughts are challenging to control, try mastering your emotions; if you feel your emotions are difficult to control, try mastering your sexual impulses. If you can master that, then the control of the former parts comes more naturally. It's important to note, though, that men and women are usually wired differently; this is a whole topic in itself, and I'll leave a recommendation for a couple of books if you're interested in this practice.

So, the point of this last section of the book is simply to make you aware that the sexual part of us is also something to be considered in your practice, not just thoughts and emotions.

We can save sexual energy, and it can then be harnessed and redirected through breathing practices such as 'Pranayama', which is often taught in yogic teachings such as 'Brahmacharya'. Through retaining our sexual energy, and the longer we practice it, we can experience massive increases in overall energy levels; we become more energetic beings, this ultimately gives more power to our energy body too (our astral body), and not just that, but it energises your physical life as well; giving you more energy to look after your family better, tend to your business, clean the house, cook, read, exercise AND astral project all in the same day - and with energy to spare! That's how much this spiritual principle can affect the quality of your life.

Of course, this advice may not apply to everyone; some people are naturally sexually pure. However, I know that there are others out there that by using this principle, they will improve their quality of life and also their chances of astral projection tenfold. The point here is to convert sexual energy into creative energy. It is called transmutation - not repression! It is a celebration and honouring of sexuality, not a denying of it. In occult terms in alchemy, it is referred to as the act of transmuting lead into gold.

It's important to note that if you are to practice sexual transmutation, it's recommended to combine it with daily meditation and pranayama breathing exercises. Pranayama helps the energy circulate through our bodies, because if we just retain sexual energy and do nothing with it, it can build up and become stagnant or keep us awake at night by having too much of it to work with; it has to be applied productively. This energy is also the same as 'Kundalini'; our primal and vital base energy. This energy ordinarily flows downwards and outwards; however, it can flow inwards and upwards with practice, going up the spine and illuminating and healing our brain and heart. I will leave recommended books below which provide excellent exercises for this. There are also other yogic breathing practices called 'Breath of Fire', which serve the same purpose. Additionally, it's also wonderful to combine these breathing practices with meditation. For example, when you sit down for formal practice, you can do this in the order of; relaxation, then pranayama, and then meditation.

Above all, no matter what spiritual practice you are doing – ENJOY yourself. The fact that you have read this book shows you have most likely begun to awaken your own consciousness. Once you start to awaken, understanding and wisdom naturally flow your way, along with experiences of astral projection. This is a profound path to be on, don't be too hard on yourself. It is a transcendental and joyous path leading to uncharted territories of consciousness that most of humanity have not yet realised, and it is up to people like us to push these new paradigms together, ultimately helping each other to raise the vibration of our fellow people—May the subtle presence of consciousness guide your way in strength, harmony and love.

> "If one is to succeed in anything, the success must come gently, with a great deal of effort but with no stress or obsession."
>
> - *Don Juan Matus (Carlos Castaneda)*

RECOMMENDED RESOURCES

Multidimensional Man by Jurgen Ziewe

Even though this is not a direct guide to astral travel, I had many experiences simply from the sheer inspiration of this book. It is simply a masterpiece, and I consider Jurgen to be one of the modern fathers of out of body exploration into the afterlife amongst astral projection authors. If you're looking for inspiration to achieve profound experiences, this is it. If you enjoy this book, you will love his books that he released after this one, which also focus on meditation and the awakening of consciousness.

Hacking the Out of Body Experience by Robert Peterson

This is one of the most comprehensive books on different OBE techniques. If you're looking for a book filled with various methods, that also has a scientific approach, this is it.

The Power of Now by Eckhart Tolle

Although this is not explicitly about astral projection, this book teaches the core and fundamental principles about overcoming the ego and becoming deeply present in daily life. If you can work with what is taught in this book, it can be one of the best practical teachings for awakening consciousness, and you can easily apply the skills learned from here towards Astral projection.

Advanced Yoga Practices by Yogani (aypsite.com)

This is a wonderful directory of easy to read authentic meditation and yoga practices. I highly recommend this if you're looking for more exercises to incorporate into your meditative practice. It also teaches genuine sexual cultivation and pranayama under its 'Tantra' directory.

Taoist Secrets of Love: Cultivating Male & Female Sexual Energy by Mantak Chia

These are two different books if you search for them. One is for men, and the other is for women. They provide in-depth rationale and practices for harnessing sexual energy - highly recommended if you're interested in practising what I've mentioned about this topic.

Teachings of Don Juan by Carlos Castaneda

This book is written by an American anthropologist who meets a Native American shaman who takes him as an apprentice and teaches him. If you're after a more mystical approach, this is your book. It is filled with tons of profound wisdom which applies directly to our perception of the world. If you enjoy this book, you'll like his books that were released afterwards. My Gnostic teacher knew Don Juan and his family as he lived in the same village as them in Sonora, Mexico.

Don Juan and the Art of Sexual Energy: The Rainbow Serpent of the Toltecs by Merilyn Tunneshende

If you enjoy the Carlos Castaneda books, I highly recommend reading books by Merilyn Tunneshende. She was Don Juan's second apprentice, who was much more successful and enlightened in understanding his teachings. This book also provides fascinating step-by-step dreaming exercises as well as shamanic sexual energy practices.

CONTACT ME

Thank you for reading! I hope you enjoyed the book and that you found it helpful. Since writing the book, I have also created a YouTube channel where I will continue to teach about Astral projection for free. The channel is called Astral Doorway. I will also be sharing and describing my future experiences on there.

www.youtube.com/c/AstralDoorway

I'm more than happy to answer any of your questions about any of the points made in this book, or if you just have any other type of general question. Please feel free to email me.

gene.hart@hotmail.com

Alternatively, you can leave comments on any of my videos and I will get back to you. I may even create a video to answer your question in-depth.

Wishing you ever-growing wisdom and understanding,

Gene Hart

Printed in Great Britain
by Amazon

72467131R00098